WHETHER YOU LIKE TO BLAST OR STOMP, BOMB OR CHOMP, THERE'S A VIDEO GAME JUST MADE FOR YOU

And now Ken Uston, master of Vegas casinos and video arcades alike, cues you in to all the perils and pitfalls, little-known tricks, and score-building strategies that can help make you a champ at any of the top sixteen video games being played across the nation. You'll learn when to gobble and when to run, as you scurry frantically around the mystifying PAC-MAN™ maze. You'll find out how to dodge aliens, bullets, and deadly exploding spikes while you ride out the TEMPEST™ long enough to blast the enemy right out of the universe. You'll be ready to zoom through space, targeting in to take the STAR CASTLE™ by storm, as you discover the winning techniques that can add up to big, big scores and hours of playing fun.

SCORE!

BEATING THE TOP
16 VIDEO GAMES

Brain teasers from SIGNET

SCORE!

BEATING THE TOP 16 VIDEO GAMES

KEN USTON

A SIGNET BOOK

NEW AMERICAN LIBRARY

TIMES MIRROR

PAC-MAN, MS. PAC-MAN, GALAGA, and GALAXIAN are
 trademarks of Midway Manufacturing Company.
DEFENDER, STARGATE, and MAKE TRAX are trademarks of
 Williams Electronics, Inc.
ASTEROIDS, TEMPEST, and CENTIPEDE are trademarks of
 Atari, Inc.
SPACE INVADERS and QIX are trademarks of Taito America
 Corp.
SCRAMBLE is a trademark of Stern Electronics, Inc.
STAR CASTLE is a trademark of Cinematronics, Inc.
DONKEY KONG is a trademark of Nintendo of America, Inc.
FROGGER is a trademark of Gremlin Industries, Inc.

This book has been neither authorized nor endorsed by any of the
manufacturing companies listed above.

SIGNET, SIGNET CLASSICS, MENTOR, PLUME, MERIDIAN and NAL BOOKS
are published by The New American Library, Inc., 1633 Broadway, New York,
New York 10019

First Printing, March, 1982

1 2 3 4 5 6 7 8 9

PRINTED IN THE UNITED STATES OF AMERICA

To my father
Senzo Usui

To my mother
Elsie Lubitz Usui

To my piano teacher
Erroll Garner

I would like to acknowledge the fact that the last six weeks constituted the most intense work period of my life—and there have been some biggies.

My thanks to Raymond Chan Ngok Chung, to Steve Thornock, and to aspiring CENTIPEDE® expert, Stacey Shub.

Contents

A Note
to the Reader

The objective of this book is to help you increase your playing time, while having even more fun in the arcade. The book will tell you how to improve on the arcade games you play the most. We'll discuss the hand controls of each game and idiosyncrasies and little-known facts of the game. We'll provide you with playing tips and strategies that should allow you, with some study and the initial investment of a few quarters, to rack up higher scores, to amaze your friends with your newfound skills, and perhaps even to attain some record scores.

SCORE !

BEATING THE TOP 16 VIDEO GAMES

1. SAVING QUARTERS AND BECOMING A GOOD PLAYER

Often arcadians walk up to a new game, become enthralled by the graphics or the design of the machine, throw in a quarter, and start playing. This is absolutely the worst way to become introduced to a game.

A major objective of this book is to have you get "more bang for your buck," or more appropriately "more quantity for your quarter." So, for starters, this section discusses a few things you should do before putting your quarter into a machine (some arcades accept only tokens, rather than quarters, but we'll stick with the term "quarter," knowing it applies equally to both).

It will be tempting for many of you to ignore this advice. After all, when that urge to play sets in—we've all felt it (that's why they call us addicts)—you want to get that game started as soon as possible.

But if you exercise the discipline necessary and follow the few preliminary steps outlined in this chapter, your quarters will go farther. In the long run, you'll get far more play—and have far more fun—for a given number of quarters.

Here are the steps that a responsible, rational videophile (if there is such a thing) should follow.

Watch a New Game for a While

When you first play a new game, your initial goal is not to set record scores, but to learn how to play the machine. There are dozens of different machines, each with a fairly complex set of rules, player and enemy movements, and scoring variations.

There is no way in the world that you will be able competently to play a game cold—that is, by just walking up, plopping in a quarter, and playing.

If you try this, the chances are your quarter will last only a few seconds, as you struggle with the controls and try to find out what's happening.

The first thing to do before playing a new game is to watch someone else play it for four or five (or more) games. As you do this, note several things as best as you can:

• How the player's man moves and how the controls make him move that way.

• How the enemy moves.

• The most serious threat(s) from the enemy (usually some form of "bomb" or "missile").

• Which player accomplishments account for the highest point scores and which account for lower point scores.

Obviously by just watching a few games, you won't have an in-depth knowledge of the above factors, but you will start to learn the concept of the game.

If the game is in this book (and there's a good chance it will be), you should pull it out, after watching for a while, and read about the rudiments of the game. Read the discussions of the Controls, the Board, and Characteristics right now. Don't worry about the Strategies section. That comes later.

So Step 1 is:

• Watch the game for a while.

• Read the sections on Controls, the Board, and Characteristics.

Getting a Game for Your Quarter

OK. You've watched the game for a while, read about it, and are now ready to play. The first thing to do is to ensure that you get a game credit for your quarter.

Video games, like any machines—cars, lawnmowers, airplanes, blenders, coin telephones—occasionally go on the blink. Sometimes out-of-order signs are posted on the games.

Too often these signs are too small to spot readily. Look for these signs. If you spot one, believe it. Don't throw a quarter in, hoping that maybe the machine will work this time. It may, but the odds are against you. The sign probably wasn't put up until several poor souls lost their money and finally, exasperated and frustrated, reported it to the arcade operator.

The next thing to do is check out the machine. Work the control knobs. Are they tight and solid? Or do they jiggle, rattle, or feel loose? If the latter, you're better off trying to find another machine of the same game (arcades often have more than one of the more popular games). This is particularly true of your early games when it's essential that you get a valid initial feel for the game.

If your "fix" for a game is really strong, go ahead and try to struggle with the inadequate controls. But remember, your quarter could well be wasted.

Take a look at the screen. Is the glass clean and can you see the screen clearly? Too often, especially in brightly lighted arcades, the games are placed so that there's a blinding glare on the screen from the overhead lights. Believe me, such a glare accounts for countless "blown" men and depressingly low scores.

Make sure the machine is the game it's supposed to be. Is the game really PAC-MAN®—or is the title spelled slightly differently? Does the game board look like the one in this book—or are there slight, suspicious variations? If the game is a counterfeit, there's a chance it is not nearly as smoothly running as the original. The counterfeit models are often put together on a shoestring by some fast-buck operator somewhere.

Let's assume there's no out-of-order sign and the game is the real thing and in good repair. Time to invest your quarter. If you don't see a "1" displayed next to the CREDIT indicator, don't panic or despair. The first thing to do is push the coin-release button. Every machine has one, and they often work. In fact, every once in a while (as in coin phones) you'll find you'll get two or more quarters back, as quarters from previous players were stuck in the machine (it doesn't happen so often that I'd recommend trying to make a living this way, however).

If the coin-release button doesn't work, report it to the operator. If you're in an arcade, the chances are excellent that you'll either be given a refund or the operator will open the front of the machine with a key and push the lever necessary to get you your credit(s).

It's a little riskier in a crowded bar or restaurant. Sometimes, in fact, the personnel might say, "I don't have nuthin' to do with the machine." In that case, be philosophical. Your quarter's lost. But to show consideration for the players after you, make sure an out-of-order sign is put up. Someday you may save some quarters because someone else cared enough to take this action.

Vegas Shock. If you've ever been to Las Vegas and walked down a carpeted corridor to a hotel room, chances are that when you touched the doorknob to your room, you've gotten a mild shock. This is because the static electricity there is so high.

Alas, this factor is also prevalent in Vegas video games. If you touch a quarter to a metallic part of the machine (usually the side of the coin slot), more often than not a little spark is created and the game goes into its test pattern. This is good news and bad news. The good news is that the test pattern is often pretty and colorful. The bad news is that you do not get a credit for your quarter.

Vegas Shock is not restricted to Vegas. It happens around the country—particularly when the floor around the machine is carpeted and during the colder months. But there's an easy way to avoid losing your quarter.

When putting the quarter into a game, first hold it against the coin slot for a second. If nothing happens on the screen, everything is OK. But if weird-looking patterns start forming, don't release the quarter. Keep on holding it there until the pattern has been completed and the "normal" screen display has returned. Then drop the quarter, and you'll get credit for the game.

Mid-game Vegas Shock. Even more frustrating is when the machine goes into its test pattern in the middle of a game—

particularly a game when you have a chance of either setting a bar or arcade record or getting a new personal high score. (I've yet to meet a player who didn't know his high scores on most games. The most commonly asked arcade question is "What's your high score?") This is also frustrating when you have the record score indicated on the game screen, because Vegas Shock eradicates all records noted on the screen—it's just like pulling the plug on the machine.

Mid-game Shock can happen when someone puts a quarter on the game surface to reserve the next game. But worse yet, it can also happen without apparent cause, as if a result of divine intervention. There's nothing to do about this except not to play the game anymore. Again it's advisable to make sure a sign is put up—I'd suggest "Out of Order—Mid-game Shock."

Becoming a Good Player

Let's say you've taken all the steps discussed so far and have now played a dozen or so games on your new addiction. You feel comfortable with the controls and have a fairly good feel for how your man and the enemy move and what actions rack up the most points. Now it's time to study the game in greater depth.

Leave the machine for a while, as hard as that might be. Read the Control, Board, and Characteristics sections again to ensure that you understand the points made (information referring to later boards of the game are irrelevant to you now—you want only to learn how to get through the first board of the game).

Then read the Strategies section. Much of it should now make sense to you. Some of it will not, since you haven't yet encountered advanced strategy situations.

Then return to the machine and gradually try to apply your knowledge of the game and its strategies. You'll note your scores gradually mounting, although it probably won't be a smooth climb—more like three steps forward and one step back. Even after much experience an occasional dismal game will creep in. Your scoring progress will probably look something like this:

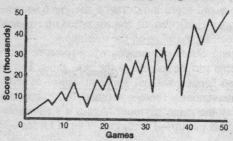

Figure 1-1

Typical Player Scoring Progress

The player will not become expert until:

• He can move the controls totally automatically, just as one steers a bicycle or car.

• He has an almost subconscious knowledge of the layout of the board and the movement of the men and the enemy.

This is good news for the manufacturer, because there is no way this can happen unless a player spends a few hours (and thus quarters) at the game.

When you finally complete the first board, and the second board appears, you may find yourself panicking again. In nearly all games, later boards are more difficult to complete than earlier boards. The player should repeat the learning process by observing the new movements of the man and the enemy. Then he should refer to the Advanced Strategy section in the chapter on the game. Chances are some of the statements that were gibberish at first now will begin to make sense.

And so the process continues for subsequent boards. You won't automatically become an expert at all the games. Let's face it, we all have different aptitudes. Some of us excel at DEFENDER® and are total klutzes at CENTIPEDE®. Other expert PAC-MAN players don't stand a chance at GALAGA®. Obviously to have fun, you should play the games you enjoy the most.

Selecting Your Game(s).

As you will see, there is wide variation in the action, controls, and theme underlying the arcade games. Some games last lots longer than others. The following table summarizes the degree of complexity of the controls in the games.

Figure 1-2

Complexity of Game Controls

Game control complexity rating	Game	Number of controls
Low	PAC-MAN®	1
	MS. PAC-MAN®	1
	FROGGER®	1
	MAKE TRAX®	1
Average	DONKEY KONG®	2
	GALAGA®	2
	GALAXIAN®	2
	CENTIPEDE®	2
	TEMPEST®	3
	SPACE INVADERS®	3
	QIX®	3
	SCRAMBLE®	3
High	STAR CASTLE®	4
	ASTEROIDS®	5
Very High	DEFENDER®	6
Highest	STARGATE®	7

2. PLAYING TIPS, ARCADE ETIQUETTE, AND USE OF THIS BOOK

The arcade games require mental, physical, and psychological preparation for top performance.

Concentration is probably the most important factor. When playing, think *only* of your game. Try to be aware in advance of what moves you may be called upon to make. Continually be aware of where the enemy is and what he is likely to do.

Do not allow yourself to be distracted. Do not talk to others or check out the players next to you. Many, many players have told me that they have been approached by someone with a question, or just a greeting, only to lose a man immediately thereafter. This has happened to me on numerous occasions.

We all play best when well rested, alert, and eager to play. Some of my worst games have been when tired, hung over, or just not up for it. The video game scores will reflect how prepared you are. A Las Vegas poker player I know has a habit of playing several games of PAC-MAN™ in an arcade near his home. If he does well, he goes out to play poker; if he does poorly, he goes home.

It's difficult to play video games well when drinking. Some of my most dismal games were played after a few martinis. Also, a player's skill tends to deteriorate after a long playing session. It's as if after a while we get video'd out.

When playing, I bend my knees. This seems to prevent me from getting too comfortable and losing concentration on the game. Many seem to play best when competing—the flowing adrenaline speeding up our reaction time and pushing us to greater achievement.

Arcade Etiquette

When a machine is occupied, you can ensure getting an opportunity to play a subsequent game by putting up a quarter. There may be quarters lined up in front of yours, which indicates when your turn will come.

But be considerate. Don't reach in front of the player when putting up your quarter, blocking his view of the screen. If his ship gets blasted, he may retaliate by blasting you. Put your quarter up in between the player's boards, if possible, while he's waiting for the new board to appear. The least distraction or lapse in concentration, as I said, can lead to video disaster.

Don't talk to the player or ask him questions about the game. If he offers information, fine. But don't distract him. He may try to be a nice guy and respond to your queries, as he loses man after man. But it's not fair to him.

Don't inadvertently jostle or brush against the player. On several occasions this has happened to me. It seems that the annihilation of my man nearly always coincides with my checking to see if I've been pickpocketed.

If you're playing alone and someone puts up a quarter for the next game, it's OK to ask, "OK if I play the next game with you?"

If he says no, however, be understanding. There are times, in such games as SPACE INVADERS™, when the movements in the game are altered by two-player games—to the detriment of predetermined strategies. Further, some players prefer the intense concentration of playing all their men consecutively. I find that this tends to lead to better scores.

Use of This Book

The next 16 chapters describe the most popular video games. For each game, I have included the following:

1. BASIC OBJECTIVE

     A one- or two-sentence summary of what you, the player, should try to accomplish.

2. SCENARIO

The basic plot of the game as dreamed up by its creators.

3. NOVICE, GOOD, AND EXPERT SCORES

4. CONTROLS

A complexity rating and a description and diagram of the knobs and buttons that operate the machine.

5. THE BOARD

A description and diagram of the layout of the game board.

6. CHARACTERISTICS

Scoring and Number of Men

How You Lose

Facts You Should Know

7. STRATEGIES

Beginning Strategy

Advanced Strategy

8. OTHER VERSIONS OF THE GAME (where applicable).

Definitions

Man and ship. The manufacturers have come up with a variety of space-age terms for the player's entity in the games, such as "laser base," "blaster," "humanoid," etc. To minimize the confusion, I will usually refer to our player-hero as "man" or "ship" (e.g., "move your man quickly to the left" or "the game gives you an extra ship at 10,000 points").

Alien. The enemy is also identified by various terms such as "invader," "galaxian," and "warbird." In many cases, I will call these entities "aliens."

Bomb. Aliens often shoot at our man with "laser blasts," "missiles," and other intimidating ammunition. I generally refer to these threats as "bombs."

Board. In each game, the player has a mission to complete. When this is done, the player is generally assigned another mission, usually more difficult. I refer to the first mission as the "first board" of the game and to subsequent missions as the "second board," "third board," etc. Thus, QIX™, DONKEY KONG™, and MAKE TRAX™ all have first, second, and subsequent boards, even though their screen configurations are quite different from one another.

Game. When the player has lost his last man, the game is finished and a "game over" message is generally displayed. On occasion, the player may continue in the next game to advanced boards by inserting another quarter. "Game" refers to the play that takes place during one quarter.

Turning the game over. Players have become so expert at some of the games that they often exceed the highest recordable score on the machine. The game's scoring mechanism then resets to zero. Arcadians call this "turning the game over."

You now know the steps you should take to save quarters and to become a good player, and how to use this book. With study, a few quarters, and some practice, you will find your game scores beginning to mount.

On the following page is a video-graph to record your progress at the games. Plot your high score in each game by filling in the bars—preferably with a colored felt-tip pen. Use the scale at the base of each bar; the numbers represent thousands of points.

As you improve, you can extend the length of each bar on the graph. This will enable you to visually check your progress, as you go from novice to good and, maybe, to expert in the games.

So study well and go set some records!!

Figure 2-1

Video-Graph: "What's Your High Score?"

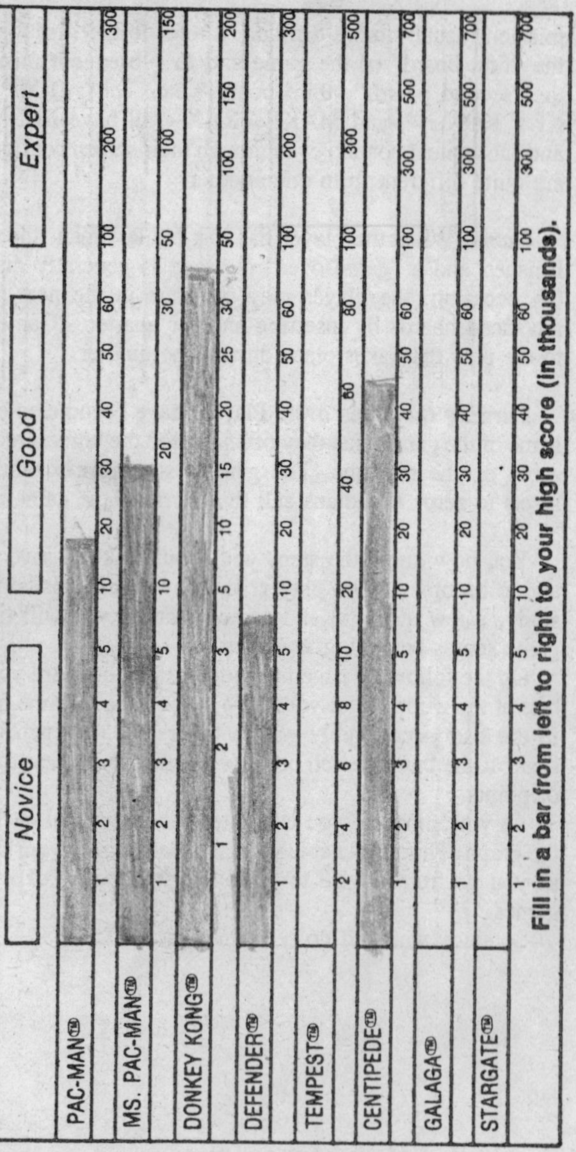

	Novice	Good	Expert
PAC-MAN™	1 2 3 4 5 10 20	30 40 50 60	100 200 300
MS. PAC-MAN™	1 2 3 4 5 10	20 30	50 100 150
DONKEY KONG™	1 2 3 5 10	15 20 25 30	50 100 150
DEFENDER™	1 2 3 5 10 20	30 40 50	100 200 300
TEMPEST™	1 2 3 4 5 10 20	30 40 50 60	100 200 300
CENTIPEDE™	2 4 6 8 10 20	30 40 50 60	80 100 300 500
GALAGA™	1 2 3 4 5 10 20	30 40 50 60	100 300 500 700
STARGATE™	1 2 3 4 5 10 20	30 40 50 60	100 300 500 700

Fill in a bar from left to right to your high score (in thousands).

Video-Graph (cont.)

	Novice	Good	Expert
QIX™	1 2 3 4 5	10 20 30 40 50	100 200 300
FROGGER™	2 5	10 15 20	40 60 80 100
MAKE TRAX™	1 2 3 4 5	10 20 30 40 50	100 200 300
ASTEROIDS™	1 2 3 4 5	10 20 30 40 50	100 300 500 700
SCRAMBLE™	1 2 3 4 5	10 20 30 40 50	75 100
GALAXIAN™	1 2 3 4 5	10 20 30 40 50	100 300 500 700
STAR CASTLE™	1 2 3 4 5	10 20 30 40 50	100 300 500 700
SPACE INVADERS™	2	10 15 20 25	50 75 100

Lengthen bars as your high scores mount.

3. THE LEADER OF THE PAC: PAC-MAN™

PAC-MAN is currently the country's favorite video game. Players are putting almost 50 million quarters into PAC-MAN machines each week. Manufacturers, aware of this, are producing numerous games with similar themes, but the players seem to keep playing PAC-MAN.

1. Basic Objective

• To eat the dots in a maze, avoiding pursuing monsters.
• Also, to eat the monsters when they're vulnerable and to eat successively higher-valued symbols that appear with each board.

2. Scenario

You are PAC-MAN, a friendly-looking yellow circle with a little wedge missing. You travel through a maze, eating dots in your path, and are pursued by four ravenous monsters. If any of them catches you, you're a goner.

There are four "energizers," one in each corner of the maze. If you hit the energizers, the monsters are rendered helpless and you can "eat" them, making them disappear for a few seconds.

If you eat all the dots on the board, you are rewarded with another board, in which the monsters move even faster. Ah, the endless travails of the hapless PAC-MAN.

3. Novice, Good, and Expert Scores

Novices generally score around 1,000 to 3,000 points.

Players with some experience score in the 7,000 to 12,000 range, and good players score 30,000 to 70,000 points.

Experts reach from 100,000 to 300,000, and real pros turn the game over (the highest score handled by the machine is 999,990) and have scored as high as 3.1 million points.

Controls

Complexity rating: Low.

PAC-MAN controls are as simple as those of any of the video games. There is a four-directional joystick, or knob, in the center of the control board which the player moves either up, down, right, or left.

Figure 3-1

The Grip

It's best to hold the knob loosely, between the thumb and the index and middle finger. Use a light touch, although the excitement of the game often makes this difficult. This is why such maladies as "PAC-MAN finger" (a not insignificant callus on the side of the first joint of the middle finger) and "PAC-MAN shoulder" (a dull pain in the shoulder joint) are not uncommon.

Some players surround the knob with the hand, holding it tightly against the palm of the hand. Such a grip makes for slow, uncoordinated movements. A lighter grip allows the player to maneuver PAC-MAN quickly and deftly.

5. The Board

The configuration of the PAC-MAN board never changes from board to board.

Figure 3-2

PAC-MAN™ Board Layout

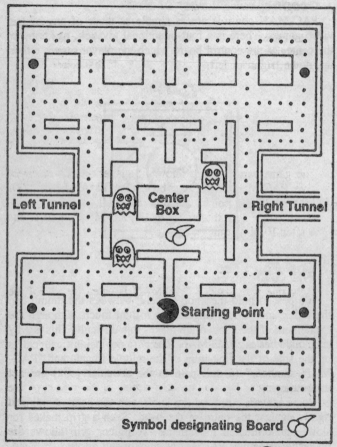

The board consists of 240 dots placed in mazelike paths, with four energizers, one in each corner. There are two tunnels, one on the left and one on the right of the board, through which PAC-MAN or the monsters may go.

6. Characteristics

Scoring and Number of Men

Each dot eaten:	10 points
Each energizer eaten:	50 points
Eating the 1st monster after an energizer is hit:	200 points
Eating the 2nd monster:	400 points
Eating the 3rd monster:	800 points
Eating the 4th monster:	1,600 points
Eating the symbol:	100 to 5,000 points

The game can be set to allow the player one, two, three, or five PAC-MEN, with one bonus PAC-MAN at 10,000, 15,000, or 20,000 points, or no bonus at all.

Most games give the player three PAC-MEN and a bonus man after 10,000 points.

How You Lose

Only one way—when PAC-MAN is eaten by one of the monsters.

Facts You Should Know

The monsters. The monsters enter the board one by one at the beginning of each play from a box in the center of the board. Each of the monsters has a name, a nickname, and movement characteristics (see the next page).

The first monster out of the center box is Shadow. He immediately heads for the northeast quadrant of the board.

Color	Name	Nickname	Characteristics
Red	Shadow	Blinky	Follows PAC-MAN around the maze
Pink	Speedy	Pinky	Fast; can out run PAC-MAN on straightaways.
Blue	Bashful	Inky	Backs off and turns into an intersection if threatened by PAC-MAN.
Orange	Pokey	Clyde	Often does the wrong thing, like taking the wrong turn when following PAC-MAN

PAC-MAN starts in the lower portion of the board. This is significant, as we will see.

After PAC-MAN hits an energizer, the monsters change direction. While in their vulnerable "blue state," the monsters are quite elusive and change directions in unpredictable ways.

When PAC-MAN goes through one of the tunnels, the monsters, if following, slow down. The monsters may catch PAC-MAN on the straightaways, but if PAC-MAN makes a series of turns, he will outrun the monsters.

Safe and dangerous areas. PAC-MAN is safest when he's away from any of the chasing monsters. He's also safe when near an energizer, even with monsters in proximity, because he may readily eat the energizer and render the monsters helpless.

The most dangerous areas are the southernmost long channel and the four corners of the board. This is because PAC-MAN may be surrounded by monsters attacking from two sides.

Successive boards. When all the dots and energizers are eaten, a new board appears. The characteristics of each new board change in three ways:

1. The value of the symbol when eaten

These values increase for successive boards, as follows:

Figure 3-3

Symbols of Each Board
and Maximum and Reasonable Scores

Board Number	Symbol (Fruit)	Symbol Name	Points to Player When Fruit Is Eaten	Maximum Possible Score*	Reasonable Score**
1		Cherries	100	14,800	8,000
2		Strawberry	300	30,000	15,000
3		1st Orange (also Peach)	500	45,600	20,000
4		2d Orange	500	61,200	24,500
5		1st Apple	700	77,200	30,000
6		2d Apple	700	93,200	35,000
7		1st Pineapple (also Grape)	1,000	109,800	43,000
8		2d Pineapple	1,000	126,400	47,500
9		1st Bird (also Phoenix & Galaxian)	2,000	145,000	54,000
10		2d Bird	2,000	163,600	60,500
11		1st Bell (also Beehive)	3,000	184,200	70,000
12		2d Bell	3,000	204,800	78,500
13		1st Key	5,000	229,400	91,000
14		2d Key	5,000	254,000	103,400
15		3d Key	5,000	278,600	115,800
16 and beyond		Keys	5,000		150,000 to 1,000,000 +

*Unattainable since the player will never eat all four blue monsters four times each board.
**Based on reasonably proficient play of the Fast Game.

Figure 3–3 also shows maximum and reasonable scores for each board.

2. *The speed of PAC-MAN and the monsters*

The second characteristic that changes in successive boards is the speed of the men. In earlier boards, PAC-MAN and the monsters move slowly. As the boards progress, both increase

Figure 3-4

Slow- and Fast-Game Equivalents and Blue-Monster Time

Slow-Game Board	Equivalent to Fast-Game Board	Blue-Monster Duration ("Blue Time")
1. Cherries	X*	Very long
2. Strawberry	1. Cherries	Very long
3. 1st Orange	X*	Very long
4. 2d Orange	2. Strawberry	Long
5. 1st Apple	3. 1st Orange	Medium
6. 2d Apple	X*	Very long
7. 1st Pineapple	4. 2d Orange	Medium
8. 2d Pineapple	5. 1st Apple	Short
9. 1st Bird	6. 2d Apple	Short
10. 2d Bird	7. 1st Pineapple	Very long
11. 1st Bell	8. 2d Pineapple	Medium
12. 2d Bell	9. 1st Bird	Short
13. 1st Key	10. 2d Bird	Short
14. 2d Key	11. 1st Bell	Medium
15. 3d Key	12. 2d Bell	Short
16. 4th Key	13. 1st Key	Short
17. 5th Key	14. 2d Key	NO blue
18. 6th Key	15. 3d Key	Short
19. 7th Key	X*	NO blue
20. 8th Key	X*	NO blue
21. and beyond. Keys	16. and beyond. Keys	NO blue

*No equivalent on the Fast Game.

in velocity. In later boards, PAC-MAN moves slowly while the monsters move rapidly.

In the original game, the monsters initially moved quite slowly; we will call this the Slow Game. As players became more proficient and occupied the machine for longer and longer periods, the game was set with a faster initial velocity; we will call this the Fast Game. There is a direct correlation between the velocities and movements of the men in the Slow Game and the Fast Game, which is shown in Figure 3-4.

The player can tell the difference between the Slow Game and the Fast Game, as follows.

Slow Game: In the sample pattern shown on the screen before play begins, PAC-MAN eats three energizers and ends up being eaten by the light-blue monster just *above* the south-west energizer.

Fast Game: In the sample pattern, PAC-MAN eats three energizers and ends up being eaten by the orange monster just *below* the south-west energizer.

The manufacturer has also introduced new electronic chips in which the monsters' movements are different from either the Slow or the Fast Game. The player will know immediately if this is the case by observing the sample pattern. If different from the ones described above, the game has a new chip.

3. Duration of "blue time"

For each board, there are variations in the length of time the monsters stay blue. These are also indicated in Figure 3–4.

7. Strategies

Beginning Strategy

Your initial goal should be to clear the first board.

At the start of each play (whether the beginning of a new board or not), you have spare time to clear off dots, since PAC-MAN is alone at the lower portion of the board. This is the time to clear the lower dots, particularly those in the southernmost path and dots that are far from the energizers.

Try to clear as many dots as possible before hitting energizers. But don't risk getting eaten to do this. If you're in a tight jam, head for an energizer and eat a monster or two.

Don't chase the blue monsters too far after eating an energizer. If you do, you may find yourself in danger, far from the safety of an energizer, as the monsters revert to their original aggressive state.

Use the tunnels to evade the monsters and to get clear to eat isolated dots. The monsters slow down when they follow you through the tunnel.

If you can get to the point where all that's left on the board are energizers with surrounding dots, you have it made. Just head for each energizer in turn and eat it and the nearby dots as the monsters turn helplessly blue.

Don't worry about eating the two cherries; they have a value of only 100 points each. If you can do so safely, OK, but don't take any chances.

Work the control knob so that PAC-MAN keeps moving at all times. You can do this by turning PAC-MAN in advance of approaching intersections. You'll become more adroit at this after a few games, as you become accustomed to the timing of the knob and the layout of the board.

If you clear the first board, you should score between 2,500 and 4,000 points.

Advanced Strategy

To clear advanced boards without predetermined patterns requires increasing dexterity, because the monsters move faster and turn blue for shorter periods, or in very advanced boards don't turn blue at all.

The second board of both the Slow Game and Fast Game can generally be completed by first eating many dots in the lower portion of the board. You won't be able to eat them all at the start of the board; eat as many as you can safely and then eat one of the lower energizers, giving you time to move to the upper portion of the board.

Note that if your timing is exactly the same in a given board, the monsters move identically. This is why it is possible to develop predetermined patterns of movement for each board which work every time.

Shown in Figure 3-5 is the pattern which works starting with the fifth board of the Slow Game and the third board of the Fast Game. It works for about 10 straight boards, so if you can get through the earlier boards, using the techniques described earlier, and use this pattern, you should be able to rack up scores of 100,000 and over.

This pattern doesn't work on the new chips that the manufacturer has come out with (to determine if it's applicable, check the sample pattern). But it's possible to develop patterns for most of the chips. My earlier book *Mastering PAC-MAN®* (Signet, January 1982) has exhaustive coverage of other patterns and ways to develop patterns for new chips.

Figure 3-5

Chart 1

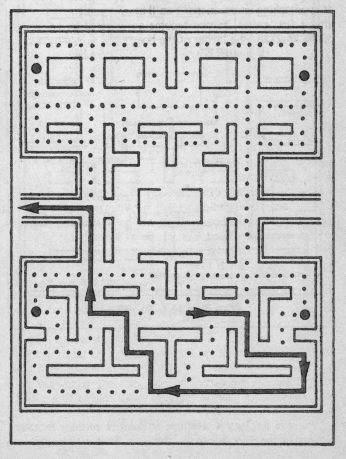

Chart 2

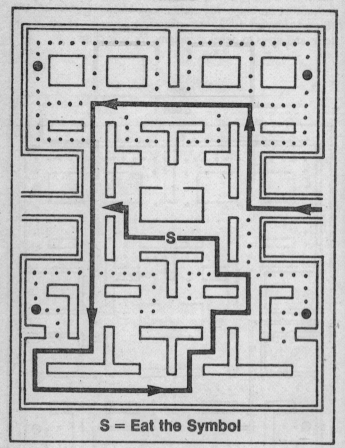

S = Eat the Symbol

Notes

Point H in Chart 4. Hesitate at Point H until the monsters are just on the other side of the energizer. Then eat the energizer

Chart 3

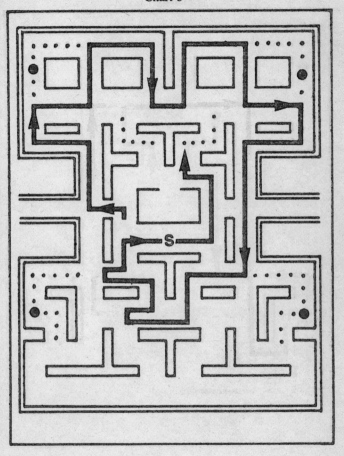

and as many blue monsters as you can (usually two or three). During boards with short blue times, don't chase the blue monsters; they will often turn color and eat PAC-MAN.

Chart 4

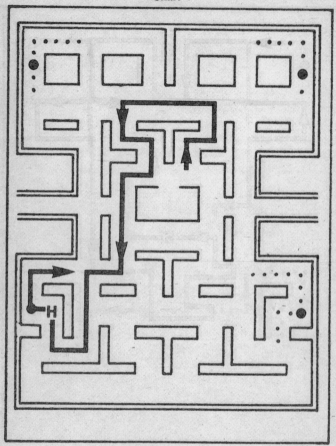

Lower Point H in Chart 5. Hesitate at Point H until the red monster is just behind you. Then, after eating the energizer, reverse to eat that monster. It's best to do this only with boards with "very long" or "long" blue times.

Chart 5

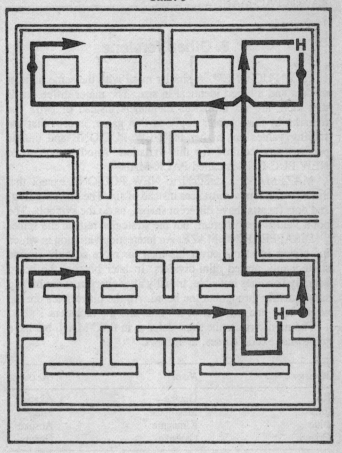

Lower Upper Point H in Chart 5. Hesitate at Point H until the monster (usually the light-blue one) has left the northwest quadrant.

This is because, after you eat the energizer, you will proceed to that quadrant, and if a monster is hanging around there, he may eat PAC-MAN.

8. Other Versions

NEW PUC-ONE®. A similar maze with the same number of dots and a board identical in size. The major difference is that there are six entrances to tunnels instead of two. The remarks in this chapter apply to this game, except that the scoring values are higher for NEW PUC-ONE and unique patterns are required for this variation. Another version of NEW PUC-ONE is called PACK-MAN®.

MAZEMAN®. Identical to NEW PUC-ONE except that there are ten tunnel entrances instead of six. The player (a frog) and dots (hearts) have different shapes, as do the symbols. The point values are different, but the strategies remain the same.

DISAPPEARING MAZE. An interesting variation in which the player must maneuver his men far more adroitly around strategically placed mini-dividers. In later boards, the board actually becomes invisible, initially after energizers are hit and subsequently throughout the board. All the player sees are the white dots, and, of course, his man and the monsters.

The monsters are the same color as in PAC-MAN, but have somewhat exotic names, as follows:

Monster	Name	Nickname
Red	Oikake	Akabei
Pink	Machibuse	Pinky
Blue	Kimagure	Aosuke
Orange	Otoboke	Guzuta

The key to playing this game is to memorize the layout of the board. This is not easy because of the mini-dividers. However, players who do so can complete just as many boards in this game as they can at conventional PAC-MAN.

4. AN A-MAZING LOVE STORY: MS. PAC-MAN™

Midway has come out with an imaginative sequel to PAC-MAN™, called MS. PAC-MAN, I would guess, to appeal to the many women who became addicted to the original game. While many of the features of MS. PAC-MAN are identical to the first version, there are significant differences which require revised playing strategies.

1. Basic Objective

As in PAC-MAN, to eat dots and avoid monsters. But the dots are laid out in several different mazes rather than in a single configuration.

2. Scenario

The player is now represented by a *female* yellow circle which gobbles dots just as rapaciously as PAC-MAN. Our heroine has a little bow in her head, flirtatiously long eyelashes, and dark-red lipstick.

Both games have brief intermissions after several boards have been completed successfully.

The PAC-MAN Interludes

Each PAC-MAN interlude becomes increasingly risqué, consistent, I suppose, with masculine predilection:

Interlude 1 (rated G). Shadow chases PAC-MAN across the screen from right to left. They disappear off the screen and appear once again. This time, Shadow (now blue in color, of course) is chased by a huge PAC-MAN, about five times his size.

Interlude 2 (rated PG). Shadow chases PAC-MAN across the screen, but his robe gets caught on an impediment. Shadow stops, looks up in bewilderment and then down at his ripped robe. A bit of below-knee bare leg is exposed.

Interlude 3 (rated R). Shadow chases PAC-MAN across the screen (his robe is still ripped). They disappear and then enter the screen once again, PAC-MAN now chasing Shadow. Shadow is holding his robe and is stark naked! What on earth took place when the two of them were offscreen?

The MS. PAC-MAN Interludes

These intermissions are closer to real show biz—a director's clapboard introduces each of them; they're labeled Act I, Act II, and Act III.

Act I: "They Meet." PAC-MAN and MS. PAC-MAN, total strangers, are separately walking down the street, pursued by their respective monsters. They approach each other, the two monsters bump heads, and the two PAC-persons continue on, arm in arm.

Act II: "The Chase." MS. PAC-MAN wildly chases PAC-MAN all over the screen, more frantically than any monster ever did (and it's not even Leap Year).

Act III: "Junior." First we see a large stork. Then there's Mr. and (I presume) Mrs. PAC-MAN with Junior, a tiny yellow PAC-child.

3. Novice, Good, and Expert Scores

• Novices score around 1,000 to 3,000 points.

• Good players score less than at PAC-MAN (because patterns don't work), from 10,000 to 30,000 points.

• Experts can still get into 6 figures, from 100,000 to around 150,000 points.

4. Controls

Complexity rating: Low.
A single four-directional joystick.

Figure 4-1

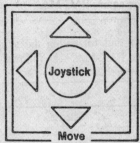

5. The Board

The configuration of the board changes every two boards. Not only that, but the monsters move differently in a given board. For this reason, improvisational ability is exceedingly important to rack up high scores at this game.

The configuration of the first three boards are shown in the Strategies section.

6. Characteristics

Scoring and Number of Ships

Each dot eaten:	10 points
Each energizer eaten:	50 points
Eating the 1st monster after an energizer is hit:	200 points
Eating the 2nd monster:	400 points
Eating the 3rd monster:	800 points
Eating the 4th monster:	1,600 points

The points awarded for eating the symbol in successive boards varies from PAC-MAN, as follows:

Board no.	Symbol	Points
1	Cherries	100
2	Strawberry	200
3	Orange	500
4	Pretzel	700
5	Apple	1,000
6	Pear	2,000
7	Banana	5,000
8	? Random	100 to 5,000

In board 8 and beyond, any one of the seven symbols may appear. The player receives points for eating the symbol in accordance with the values for each symbol, as shown above.

Most machines are set to award an extra man—uh, I mean, woman—at 10,000 points.

How You Lose

When MS. PAC-MAN is eaten by one of the monsters.

Facts You Should Know

During each board, the symbol appears in various locations and travels slowly around the board.

The board configurations change every two boards, as follows:

Board no.	Symbols	Board Configuration	Tunnels
1 & 2	Cherries & strawberry	Pink	4 tunnels, two at the top, two at the bottom
3 & 4	Orange & pretzel	Blue	4 tunnels, two at the very top row of the board
5 & 6	Apple & pear	Orange	2 tunnels in the center
7 & 8	Banana & ?	Blue #2	4 tunnels

The board configurations require different strategies.

7. Strategies

Pink board. This board is the easiest of the configurations. Predetermined patterns can still not be worked out, because the monsters move in random ways—a key difference from

PAC-MAN. During the pink board the player should concentrate on clearing out the large square around the board (Figure 4-2). In many of the pink boards, the player will be able to clear the entire square, if he starts at the very beginning of the board and moves in a counterclockwise direction. On occasion, his path will be intercepted by a monster. The player should take evasive action and, at the earliest opportunity, return to the "square" and complete clearing the dots.

The next order of business in the pink board is to clear the channels at the bottom of the board. To the extent possible,

Figure 4-2

Pink Board

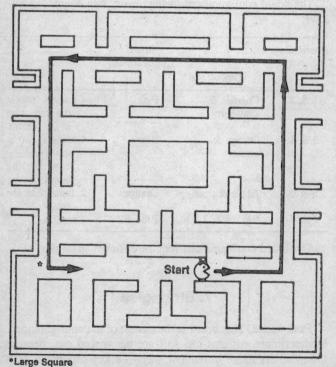

Start

*Large Square

save the energizers for the end of the board. The exception to this is when three or four monsters are grouped together and MS. PAC-MAN is near an energizer. Eat the energizer and as many monsters as you can (safely) for lots of bonus points.

Blue board (Figure 4-3). This is the most difficult of the boards to complete. Four tunnels appear, but two are on the very top row of the board. This row is far from readily accessible and cannot be used very frequently as a safety valve— notice how the paths are quite restricted at the top of the board.

Figure 4-8

Blue Board

The player can easily get caught in one of these restricted paths and be eaten by a monster meeting him from the other side.

For these reasons, the player should be defensive when ascending to the top of the board. Be sure that you have a clear path either to one of the two top energizers or to the tunnels. If you are pursued by monsters as you're improvising, stay in the lower portion of the board for your evasions. A high percentage of players' men are eaten in the upper portion of the blue board.

Orange board (Figure 4-4). The monsters move quickly and turn blue for shorter periods during the orange board.

Figure 4-4

Orange Board

While the configuration of this board is not as difficult as the previous one, there are only two tunnels. The tunnels fortunately are centrally located and provide an accessible escape hatch.

Because the movements of the monsters vary widely in any given board, improvisational skill is essential to high scores at MS. PAC-MAN. Remember that the monsters may be outrun by using the tunnels and by making a series of quick turns. Continually bear in mind also that the monsters reverse directions when you eat an energizer; you can sometimes make them move where you want them to just as they turn blue, for easy and frequent gobbling.

5. SHEER CHIVALRY: DONKEY KONG™

DONKEY KONG is currently one of the most popular video games. A poll of arcades by one magazine showed DONKEY KONG to have the highest weekly gross collections of any of the coin-operated games during the month of January 1982.

1. Basic Objective

To successfully complete as many "levels" as possible by reaching the top of a series of steel structures, avoiding the threatening objects that come your way, and eventually collapsing the final structure of each level.

2. Scenario

Your man is a heroic little carpenter named Mario. A beautiful girl is being held captive by an evil gorilla ("Donkey Kong") at the top of a 25-meter-high steel structure. You can free the gal from her captor by climbing up ladders that lead to the top of the structure. But the gorilla is throwing barrels down at you, and there are other objects that can also destroy you.

If you do reach the top, the gorilla grabs the girl and takes her to the top of another structure, also 25 meters high. The second structure has a series of beam connectors or "bridges," which you can do away with by crossing them. If you eliminate all eight of these bridges, the entire structure collapses and the gorilla falls to his death. You've won.

But wait. That's just at difficulty level 1. You go on to subsequent levels, each of which, naturally, is increasingly more difficult to complete.

3. Novice, Good, and Expert Scores

• The beginning player may be able to get through the first board (he's got three shots at it). If he does, he'll probably score around 3,000 points.

• The good player can usually complete several boards of level 2, yielding scores of around 20,000 points.

• Expert players get to level 6 (more than 20 boards and 140,000 points), and some real pros have scored in the 800,000 range.

4. Controls

Complexity rating: Average.

There is a four-directional joystick, which moves our carpenter, Mario, up, down, left, and right. It's located (I think erroneously) on the left side of the control board.

There's also a JUMP button, which causes Mario to jump (over threatening barrels or other objects). This button is on the right side of the control board.

Figure 5-1

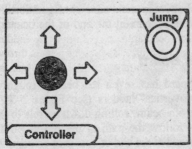

If the joystick is held in a given position, Mario will continue to move in that direction. But the JUMP button works differently—it must be pushed every time the player wants Mario to jump. Mario can jump when standing still or moving to the left or right. He cannot jump when moving vertically, either up or down. He cannot jump while wielding a hammer, either (which will be explained in a minute).

5. The Board

There are four different board configurations, which we shall refer to as:

Red	—a structure consisting of red beams
Blue	—a structure consisting of blue beams
Elevators	—a structure which has two elevators
Mud Factory	—a structure which looks like, yes, a mud factory (also called "The Coals" and "The Pie" board).

Each difficulty level (henceforth called "level") starts with a red board and ends with a blue board (after the completion of which the gorilla goes to his just deserts). In between these two boards are interspersed elevators, mud factories, or additional red boards. Figure 5-2 shows the boards, the levels, the starting bonuses, the board configurations, and the approximate average score at the end of the boards.

The Red Board

The red board has seven red beams, roughly horizontal, connected by vertical ladders (see Figure 5-3). The gorilla stands on the 6th beam, rolling down barrels to thwart Mario. Some barrels follow the path of the beams on their descent. They can descend at the end of beams or on complete or broken ladders. Others, more dangerous, fall more directly, dropping as if the beams didn't exist ("direct barrels").

Our heroine stands on the very top (7th) beam waiting to be rescued. A little "Help" message appears above her every once in a while to reveal the depths of her agony.

Figure 5-2

Boards, Levels, Configurations, and Average Scores

Board no.	Board configuration	Approximate average score at end* (thousands)
Difficulty Level 1 – Starting Bonus 5,000 Points		
1	Red	4–5
2	Blue	9–11
Difficulty Level 2 – Starting Bonus 6,000 Points		
3	Red	15–17
4	Elevators	18–24
5	Blue	29–33
Difficulty Level 3 – Starting Bonus 7,000 Points		
6	Red	32–37
7	Mud factory	39–44
8	Elevators	48–50
9	Blue	58–60
Difficulty Level 4 – Starting Bonus 8,000 Points		
10	Red	65–69
11	Mud factory	71–73
12	Red	80
13	Elevators	85
14	Blue	95
Difficulty Level 5 – Starting Bonus 8,000 Points		
15	Red	103
16	Mud factory	110
17	Red	115
18	Elevators	119
19	Red	123
20	Blue	141
Difficulty Level 6 – Starting Bonus 8,000 Points		
21	Red	149
22	Mud factory	157
23	Red	164
24	Elevators	170

Notes: *There can be wide variations in score depending upon bonuses and other playing variations.

*The starting bonus never exceeds 8,000 points.

*The first board of each level starts at "25 m," referring to the height which the player attains in clearing the board. This increases by 25 m for each board, reaching a maximum of 150 m at the 6th board of each level.

The red board has two little hammers which our man can pick up (by jumping up to them). He can then destroy the barrels by hitting them with the hammer—a good defensive measure—and it gives additional points. One or more fireballs are formed on the low beam—they're rarely much of a threat in this board.

Our goal: to avoid the barrels and climb up to the 7th beam to rescue the girl. If we succeed, a little pink heart flashes (ah,

Figure 5-3

The Red Board

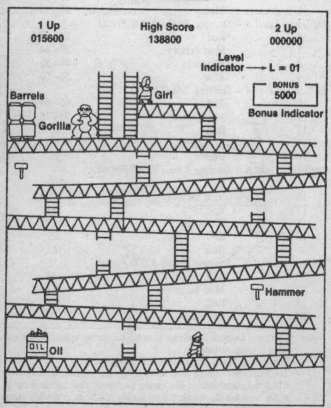

young love), but our happiness is only fleeting—because the gorilla suddenly grabs the girl, climbs up two ladders, and ascends to the top of another structure (i.e., board).

The Blue Board

The blue board is the final board of each level (which only stands to reason, because after its successful completion, the

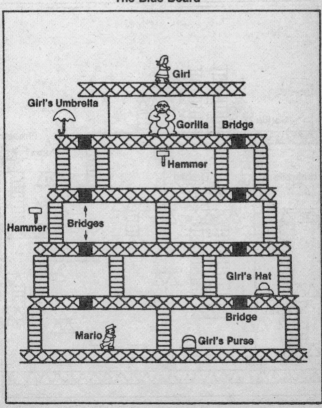

Figure 5-4

The Blue Board

gorilla falls to his death). The board has six blue beams connected by ladders (see Figure 5-4). The gorilla stands on the 5th beam and our girl is on the 6th beam.

Beams 2 through 6 each have two bridges which vanish as Mario walks or jumps over them. Fireballs appear one by one from the side of the screen and dance around the beams, threatening Mario. A maximum of five fireballs may appear on the board at any one time.

Figure 5-5

The Elevators Board

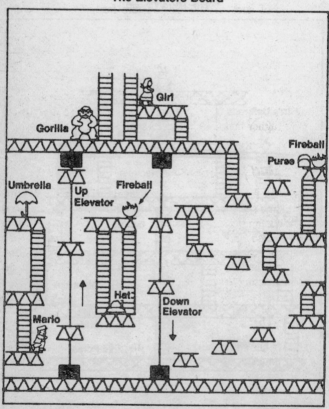

Our goal: to eliminate all eight bridges. Then the structure, unsupported, collapses and the gorilla falls to his death. Our girl is saved!! The level is over. But the engineers won't let us rest on our laurels—it's time to play the next level.

The Elevators Board

The elevators board first appears in level 2—the fourth board of the game (see Figure 5-5). The elevators have two fireballs which threaten us—one at the top moving around the isolated structure located between the two elevators, and one at the top of another isolated structure farther up and to the right.

But the big threats of this board are the bouncing hammers that start at the top and work down. They can bounce over Mario if he stands in the right spot. If not—whammo, it's all over.

It's real tough to avoid the bouncing hammers when standing on the beam occupied by the gorilla and get up to the girl on the next higher beam. But, as we shall see, it can be done.

The Mud Factory Board

The mud factory first appears at level 3 (the seventh board of the game; see Figure 5-6). Pans of mud (don't ask me why) travel back and forth on several beams, threatening Mario. There are also fireballs.

Our goal: to ascend to the 2nd beam from the top. Yes, the gorilla will then grab the girl and climb another 25 meters on another structure.

The Girl's Belongings

During her abduction by the gorilla, our girl becomes some-what disheveled. She drops her hat, purse, and umbrella, which are located at various spots during the blue, elevators, and mud factory boards (that is, on all but the red board). If Mario reaches these, we get bonus points.

Figure 5-6

The Mud Factory Board
(Also "The Coals"; "The Pies")

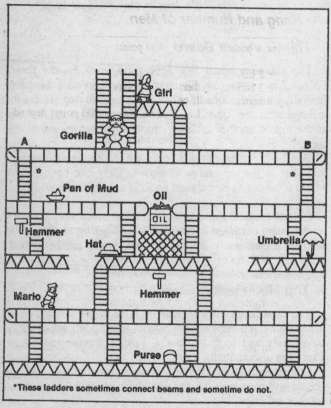

A

Girl

Gorilla

B

Pan of Mud

Oil

OIL

Hammer

Hat

Umbrella

Mario

Hammer

Purse

*These ladders sometimes connect beams and sometime do not.

6. Characteristics

Scoring and Number of Men

Jumping over a barrel, or other object:	100 points
Jumping over 2 barrels together:	300 points
Jumping over 3 barrels together:	800 points
Hammering a barrel, fireball, or pan of mud:	300, 500, or 800 points depending on how far away the object is when Mario hammers it.
Picking up the girl's hat, handbag or umbrella:	300 points in level 1, 500 points in level 2, 800 points in level 3 and beyond

The bonus. Each board starts out with a bonus that also serves as a timing device. The first four levels offer a starting bonus of 5,000, 6,000, 7,000, and 8,000 points, respectively. All subsequent boards award an 8,000 bonus.

During the play of the board, the bonus continually decrements, as indicated at the upper right portion of the screen (where the level number is also displayed). Upon completion of the board, the player receives a bonus equal to the amount remaining in the bonus at the time the board is completed. Thus there's a premium on time (don't dawdle on the ladders).

If Mario doesn't complete the board by the time the bonus has decreased all the way to zero, he meets his demise.

The player gets three Marios, with a bonus Mario, usually at 7,000, 15,000, or 20,000 points, depending on how the machine is set.

How You Lose

• By getting clobbered with a barrel, fireball, pan of mud, or bouncing hammer.

• By running into the burning containers of oil.

• By jumping off beams into space (thus falling off the structure).

• By jumping into some gap, such as an inter-beam space, off the elevator ledges, or hitting Mario's head on the structure at the top of the elevator.

• By colliding with the gorilla.

• By running out of bonus time before completing a board.

If Mario ascends a partial ladder and the joystick remains in the UP position, he will merely stop and not fall to his doom.

Facts You Should Know

The hammer. Mario can pick up the hammer by jumping up when directly under it. At that point, the fireballs turn blue and both the fireballs and barrels can be destroyed (hammered) by Mario. But be careful—the objects can still destroy Mario when he has the hammer if they collide with him. When Mario has the hammer, a special tune which brings to mind the cavalry-charge melody is played.

When Mario has the hammer, he's partially immobile, because he can't jump or move up or down ladders. After an interval, Mario loses the hammer, and the objects are no longer vulnerable to being hammered.

Jumping. The timing of the JUMP button will take a few quarters. While it's best to avoid double barrels, be assured that Mario can jump over two barrels at the same time.

Completion of the Boards. The boards are completed as follows:

Red board: when Mario gets to the highest beam (the one on which the girl is standing).

Blue board: when Mario travels on or over all eight bridges, toppling the gorilla.

Elevators board: when Mario gets to the highest beam.

Mud factory board: when Mario ascends to the 2nd-highest beam.

Waiting on the ladder. Mario can wait on the ladder and not be accosted by objects *if* he touches the beam above him. But if he waits in the middle of the ladder, barrels, and fireballs from the beam above can drop down the ladder, abruptly ending Mario's voyage.

7. Strategies

I may be weird, but I find it *much* easier to maneuver the joystick with my right hand (I'm right-handed). Thus in DONKEY KONG (as in QIX™), I cross my hands while playing, holding the joystick with my right hand and pushing the JUMP button with my left.

Try it—if you're right-handed, it may help.

Beginning Strategy

Your initial goal should be to get Mario through the first (red) board, which will give you a score of around 4,000 or 5,000 points.

There's a fairly simple approach which should accomplish this (see Figure 5-7):

1. Move Mario instantaneously to Ladder 1 ("L1"), go up L1, move to L2, and move up L2 until Mario is just barely touching the beam above him (beam 3).

2. Wait on L2 (barely touching the overhead beam, of course) while a barrel passes overhead. Then move up and get on L3.

3. Wait on L3 (guess what you must barely touch) until a barrel passes overhead. Go up to beam 4, and stand at point A.

4. Jump a barrel or two until you have breathing time to ascend L4.

5. Go up L4 and wait until there is a nice space between barrels. Then go up L4 to beam 5 and go left and jump up and get the hammer.

Figure 5-7

Strategy for the First (Red) Board

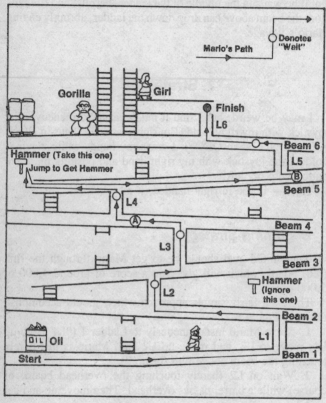

6. Then travel right (east) along beam 5, hammering barrels, until you get to point B. Keep hammering and wait at point B until you lose the hammer.

7. Go up L5. When on beam 6, jump a barrel or two until you have time to get safely to L6.

8. Go up L6 and collect your rewards (an obviously in-love girl—and a completed board).

A tip. When you get more comfortable with the controls, and want to get a little fancy, try this. When you pick up the hammer on beam 5, wait until a barrel approaches you. Jump up and get the hammer at the same time you jump over the barrel.

Advanced Strategy

The red board. Subsequent red boards can often be completed by taking a route similar to the one just described. However, completion of the board is progressively more difficult because the barrels move faster and sometimes come in combinations that can trap Mario.

After the first red board, a direct barrel is often thrown by the gorilla so that it reaches L1 at the same time Mario does. Watch out and be prepared to hesitate—or to jump—or both.

The blue board. A few quarters will be required to get the timing down for jumping over the gaps in the beams, using the joystick and JUMP button simultaneously, which is an essential skill for maneuvering Mario around this board.

The fireballs do not travel across the beam gaps, so one obvious ploy in destroying bridges is to travel across the bridge (destroying it) and immediately jump back over the gap to the original side, eluding the fireball (Figure 5-8).

Figure 5-8

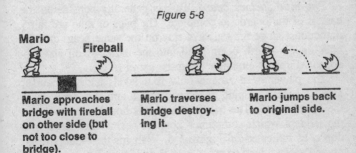

Mario Fireball		
Mario approaches bridge with fireball on other side (but not too close to bridge).	Mario traverses bridge destroying it.	Mario jumps back to original side.

The elevators board. This is generally considered the most difficult board to complete because of the rapid movement of the jumping hammers.

But notice that they generally pounce in identical spots, bouncing three times on the beam where they originate and falling straight down, as shown on Figure 5-9. Obviously this vertical channel must be avoided.

Many advanced players handle this board as follows (refer to Figure 5-9):

1. Ascend the elevator (point A) and jump back to the left-most structure (point B), pick up the umbrella, and descend again.

2. Jump on the up elevator again and then jump to the center structure (point C), get the hat, and ascend on the left side of the structure, avoiding the fireball.

3. Go across the top (point D) and jump on the down elevator.

4. Jump up onto the two structures (points E and F) and get to the beam on which the gorilla is standing, stopping at point G.

5. Let a few bouncing hammers go over your head and when the timing is right, *rush* to point H and stop (phew!!).

6. The hammers will still bounce over you. When one has *just* passed (and its position "feels" right—this is where a little intuition comes in), rush to the base of ladder L1 and get up it just as fast as you can.

The mud factory board. This is generally considered the easiest of the boards to complete. The pans of mud are fairly innocuous, since they always stay on the same beam and the ones on the fourth beam head into the barrel of oil and disappear. Fireballs emanate from the barrel of oil.

The player need ascend only four levels and, of course, avoid the pans of mud and the fireballs and stay away from the barrel of oil. The tricky part of this board is the wait for the ladders which sometimes connect beams and sometimes don't, as indicated on Figure 5-6. Wait for the ladders to go up and ascend them to point A or B on Figure 5-6, completing the board.

Figure 5-9

Strategy for the Elevators Board

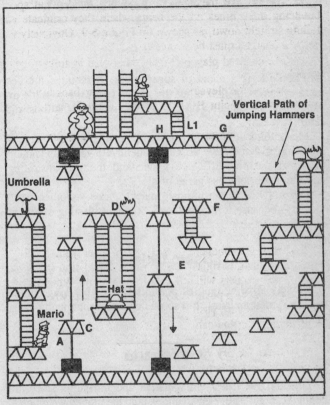

6. THE MACHO GAME: DEFENDER™

DEFENDER is a game of superlatives. It requires the best hand-eye coordination of all the games (with the possible exception of its sequel, STARGATE™), and it is the most difficult to teach.

Many think it is by far the best, most exciting, and most challenging game there is. Others believe it to be undeniably the worst, the most difficult to understand, the most frustrating, and the most pointless game of all.

DEFENDER is the ultimate macho game—women rarely play it—because it requires loud, frequent blasting of the enemy.

1. Basic Objective

To stay alive as long as possible, preferably long enough to be awarded an extra ship so one can stay continually ahead of the game.

2. Scenario

DEFENDER has an imaginative and intriguing story line behind it, but it's not easy to understand the plot by watching—or even by playing—the game.

You are in a rocket ship, flying over a planet. Standing at various locations on the planet are men, your friends, who are threatened by flying aliens. One type of alien, aptly named the lander, swoops down from the sky, plucks men off the ground, and flies away. If you shoot the lander before it reaches the top of the atmosphere (that is, the screen), you can rescue the man by then catching him in midair. You can fly on with the man or, better yet, return him safely to the ground.

Your mission is quite dangerous because there are several types of rapidly moving aliens, with different shapes, colors, and movement characteristics, that threaten to destroy your rocket ship.

If the aliens kidnap all the men, the planet disappears. You are then surrounded by hordes of one especially dangerous alien, the mutant, and your destruction is generally not far away (unless you're really good in dogfights).

After successfully fighting off several waves of attack, you are awarded a brand-new set of men (or your old friends are reincarnated—whichever you prefer) and a new planet, if the previous one was lost.

3. Novice, Good, and Expert Scores

Variation in DEFENDER scores is extreme.

• Novices have played a dozen games and never reached 1,000 points.

• Good players can score between 50,000 and 100,000.

• Experts can consistently score over 1,000,000 points. One player scored 15.9 million points in 16 hours of play; several weeks later, another player broke this record, racking up over 16 million points.

4. Controls

Complexity rating: Very high.

A two-directional joystick, moving the ship up and down, is operated with the left hand, as is a REVERSE button, which changes the direction of the ship.

The right hand must operate a FIRE button, to launch missiles at the enemy; a THRUST button, to move the ship through space; and a SMART BOMB button, which destroys all aliens which appear on the screen at the time it is pushed (with the exception of a few "swarmers," as we shall see).

For the player's third hand, located in the very center of the control board, is a HYPERSPACE button, which, when hit,

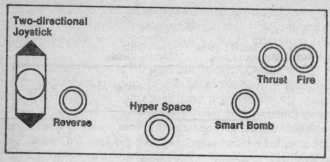

Figure 6-1

causes the player's ship to rematerialize in a new, random location on the screen.

Not only are there six controls to the game, but they must be operated with great rapidity. The fingers of an advanced player move as fast as those of a secretary typing at 100 words per minute. My friend Raymond, who's cool as a cucumber playing every other game, gets hyper while coping with DEFENDER. He wipes his brow after just about every wave. To put it in his words, "This game makes you sweat a lot."

5. The Board

The screen displays the terrain of the planet, a series of mountains and valleys, and the sky overhead. The player's ship is multi-colored and bright, as are his friends, the men. The player may fly below the surface of the terrain, as can all aliens except the landers.

At the top of the screen is a radar scanner which displays a much broader view of the planet in miniature—about eight screen-widths. The radar screen, rarely used by the novice, is a must for the advanced player. It shows the location of objects on either side of the screen so the player may react to them appropriately. The ship, men, and aliens each have a unique shape and color, both on the screen and on the radar scanner.

On the upper left of the screen is shown the number of ships and smart bombs remaining.

Figure 6-2
DEFENDER™

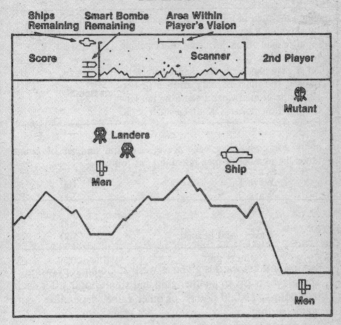

Ships Remaining   Smart Bombs Remaining   Area Within Player's Vision

Score   Scanner   2nd Player

Mutant

Landers

Men   Ship

Men

6. Characteristics

Scoring and Number of Ships

Points for shooting the aliens, as follows:

Lander:	100 or 150 points, depending on the game setting
Mutant:	150 points
Baiter:	200 points
Bomber:	250 points
Pod:	1,000 points
Swarmer:	150 points

Some games give the player 25 points for shooting his own man.

Catching the man in midair (after freeing him by shooting a lander):	500 points
Dropping a man off on the planet after catching him:	500 points
When a man lands on the planet safely by himself (he must be only an inch or two above the ground when freed from the lander—a little more is OK after a smart bomb hits):	250 points

A bonus for completing each wave, a certain number of points times the number of men remaining, as follows:

Wave 1:	100
Wave 2:	200
Wave 3:	300
Wave 4:	400
Wave 5 and beyond:	500

A consolation award is given as well: 25 points for crashing.

The player is given another ship and smart bomb after each 10,000 points, 12,000 points, or other value, depending upon the game setting.

The player is given a new set of men and a new planet after the fourth wave and every additional five waves are completed successfully (i.e., after the 9th, 14th, 19th, 24th, etc. waves). This, too, can vary depending upon the game setting.

How You Lose

By being hit by any of the aliens or their missiles.

Facts You Should Know

1. *The shape and color of objects on the screen and on the radar*

Object	Shape	Color on Screen	Color on Radar
Ship		Multi-colored and bright	Bright white
Men		Green, pink and orange	Gray
Landers		Green with an orange top	Green on bottom, orange on top
Mutants		Green with a purple middle	Green on bottom; red on top; blue on top or in middle; flashing
Baiters		Green; orange in the middle	Two green lines
Bombers		Blue and purple	Purple
Pods		Purple and blue	Multi-colored, flashing
Swarmers		Reddish-orange	Reddish-orange

2. Number and characteristics of aliens

Alien	No. of aliens in WAVE				Characteristics
	1	2	3	4+	
Lander	15	20	20	20	Fire white missiles. Do not chase ship. Turn into Mutants when reach top of screen with man.
Mutant	Depends on Landers				Tend to attack at top of screen. Chase ship from above and below. Fire shots. Make a buzzing noise, as they dodge and weave crazily.
Baiter	Depends on speed of completing the wave				Fire white missiles. Make a hissing noise. Can leave screen at top and appear at bottom, and vice versa. Faster than ship at full speed.
Bomber	0	3	4	9	Move diagonally, but slowly. Leave deadly x-shaped "mines" on screen.
Pod	0	1	3	4	Move vertically on screen. Leave Swarmer when hit.
Swarmer	Depends on no. of Pods hit				Fire missiles, but only in direction they're moving towards.

3. Other facts

• The game usually starts with 10 men.

• Swarmers can remain after the smart bomb is used, although all other aliens are destroyed.

• There is no limit to the number of player shots. Thus he may fire continuously by hitting the FIRE button as rapidly as possible (the lighter the touch, the more frequent the shots).

• The game can be set to have all the action (the ship and the aliens) move really fast. Combined with a 12,000-point requirement for a new ship, the game can get really tough. So pick your games carefully.

7. Strategies

Beginning Strategy

If you intend to become a serious DEFENDER player, it's essential that you get to the point where you can operate the controls by reflex. This comes only with practice and more than a few quarters.

The novice should start by concentrating on getting through the first wave:

1. At first, practice coordinating the use of the THRUST and FIRE buttons with the right hand, and operating the joystick with the left. Don't worry about reversing or hyperspacing. For a few games, make the sacrifice and forget about smart bombs, too. After a while, you might consider smart-bombing if you're surrounded by aliens and feel out of control. But remember your first goal is to get to be totally comfortable operating the THRUST, FIRE, and joystick controls.

2. Thrust slowly. If you thrust too rapidly, you won't be able to handle the action and will soon be destroyed.

3. Concentrate on shooting Landers. Landers should always be your primary target because they threaten to kidnap the men. If you destroy them quickly, you won't have Mutants or Baiters to worry about.

4. Try to keep the ship about level with the mountain tops (dodging as necessary). Landers tend to fly at that altitude a lot.

5. Don't be bashful about firing a lot, hitting the FIRE button often and rapidly. There's no limit on the number of shots or missiles and, of course, no penalty for missed shots.

6. Get used to sneaking a peak at the scanner to see what's

coming. Use of the scanner is essential to advanced play. In fact, after you've become somewhat proficient with the controls, it's worthwhile to invest a few quarters and practice shooting aliens looking *only* at the scanner.

7. After a while, you'll be able to complete the first wave; you'll score around 3,000 points or so. Then try to rescue the men after you've destroyed the Landers—you get 500 points for a rescue and 500 points for returning a man to the surface of the planet.

To rescue a man, just fly right into him. Then when you get a breather, fly down to the planet's surface and the man will automatically hop off.

Advanced Strategy

The waves get progressively more difficult. As shown earlier, there are 20 Landers in wave 2 and beyond (instead of 15 in the first wave), and Bombers and Pods start appearing. While becoming good at DEFENDER is primarily a matter of practice with the controls, you can take advantage of your knowledge of the characteristics of the aliens to expedite this process.

Landers. These aliens should always constitute our primary target, unless, of course, we're seriously threatened by other aliens. Watch the scanner for Landers picking up men and try to get to them to rescue the men. When approaching them, watch for the shots they fire and avoid them.

Mutants. Mutants track our ship. They often hang around the top of the screen. Either fly to the top of the screen and shoot at them while moving slightly vertically, or (as is the best strategy for Bombers) fly ahead of them, hit REVERSE, and blast them.

Baiters. These aliens are fast and evasive. Listen for a hiss, look in the scanner for the location of the Baiter, and blast them as soon as possible.

Bombers. These aliens leave a trail of little white X's which can destroy your ship. So don't fly right behind them. Get on either (vertical) side of them (avoiding the X's), pass them, reverse, and blast them. Assign Bombers a higher shooting priority in later waves, because they start leaving more X's, which can be a real impediment in trying to maneuver to shoot other objects.

Pods. Pods tend to appear at the beginning of the third and subsequent waves—often bunched together. They're worth smart-bombing, because they have the highest point value of all aliens, 1,000 points each.

Swarmers. Swarmers are difficult to hit because they're so small. They're also numerous and fire shots. But they only shoot in the direction in which they're traveling; thus it's safer to get behind them and blast them. Swarmers can really fill up the screen; when they do, it's best to smart-bomb them.

Final Tips

Be economical in the use of smart bombs; it's best to save them for later waves.

Hyperspace should be used only in dire emergencies, because the ship is not infrequently destroyed when it rematerializes on the screen.

When in the final wave before a new set of men is awarded (usually wave 4, 9, 14, etc.), it is often advantageous to carry a man around with you and protect him, through artful dodging. If you do this successfully, you will preserve the planet (and most likely your ship).

For the million-point player: DEFENDER does some unusual things when the player approaches a score of 1,000,000. When the player reaches a score of 990,000 on a machine that awards extra men at every 10,000 points, the player is awarded extra ships that he doesn't deserve (on 12,000 extra-man machines, the cutoff is just under 1,000,000 points).

The player gets an extra ship every time he shoots something and every time he gets hit. If he smart-bombs, he gets an extra ship for every object that he destroys on the screen. The only way the ship can crash without an extra ship being awarded is to hyperspace and crash.

Then why doesn't the game go on forever? Because after 1,000,000 points, the game "turns over," starts at zero again, and for some reason no extra ships or smart bombs are awarded. Thus the strategy for the multimillion-point player is to store up as many ships and bombs as possible between 990,000 and 1,000,000 points for future use.

7. THE WRIST-ACTION GAME: TEMPEST ™

TEMPEST is a colorful, noisy game that is exciting and fast-moving. It has a bonus option that will get the mathematicians moving their pencils.

1. Basic Objective

To stay alive; to avoid enemy aliens, to prevent a collision with them, and to rack up points.

2. Scenario

The player is represented by a "shooter" that he steers around the periphery of the board. Menacing aliens of varying shapes, colors, and movement characteristics threaten to crash into the shooter and destroy it, as do bullets shot from some of the aliens. To prevent this, the player must shoot the aliens and destroy them.

Each board has a unique geometric shape and is partitioned into sectors, roughly wedge-shaped. After each board is completed (except for early boards), "spikes" explode out of various sectors. If the player keeps his shooter in a sector where there is no spike, he is allowed to progress to the next board.

3. Novice, Good, and Expert Scores

• Beginning players score between 1,000 and 10,000 points.
• Good players score between 15,000 and 75,000 points. This varies, depending on the skill level initially selected by the player (and the resulting bonus), as we shall see.

• Expert players score over 100,000. Scores of up to 500,000 are not uncommon among TEMPEST experts.

4. Controls

Complexity rating: Average.

On the right side of the control board is a control knob, which turns in either direction (clockwise or counterclockwise). This knob, extremely sensitive to the touch, directs the shooter around the rim of the board.

On the left side is a FIRE button, which should generally be held down continuously by the player to maximize the number of shots fired off. There are exceptions to this rule, when the timing of shots is critical. There can be a maximum of eight shots on the screen at one time.

Also on the left is a SUPER ZAPPER button. This button activates the "Super Zapper," which can be used twice during each board. The first Super Zap clears the board of all aliens. The second super zap is somewhat unpredictable, but often destroys the enemy alien most threatening to the player.

Figure 7–1

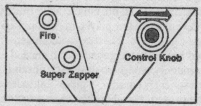

5. The Board

There are 16 different board configurations. When board 17 is reached, the cycle of configurations repeats—that is, board 17 is identical in shape to board 1, board 18 is identical to board 2, etc. The boards in later cycles are far more difficult to clear, due to the type, number, and movement of the aliens.

Figure 7–2
Second Board

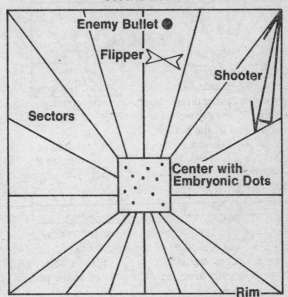

For clarity, we will define a cycle as a complete series of the 16 board configurations. Thus, cycle 1 comprises boards 1 through 16, cycle 2 comprises boards 17 through 32, etc.

The first board, the simplest to complete, is circular in shape. With one exception, the player moves the shooter clockwise or counterclockwise around the rim of the boards. In the last board of each cycle (that is, boards 16, 32, 48, 64, 80, and 96), the player moves in a figure-8 movement around the board which is shaped roughly like an infinity sign.

Shown in Figure 7–3 are the 16 shapes of the boards. These shapes are "recycled" in the same sequence six times, through board 96. Boards 97, 98, and 99 are of random shape; the player may continue beyond 99 boards, but the numbering of the boards at the top of the screen stops at 99.

Figure 7-3

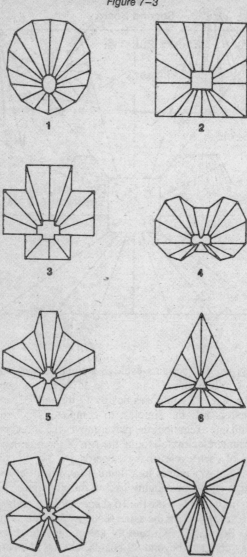

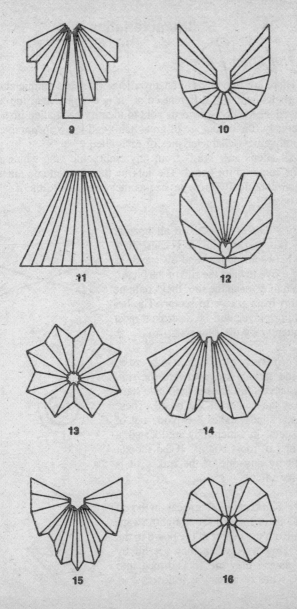

6. Characteristics

The Enemy Aliens

There are five types of enemy aliens. Each has unique characteristics and is a different color. It is essential that the advanced TEMPEST player is able to identify each alien instantaneously (the colors are of great help) and know instinctively the movement characteristics of each alien.

All aliens are "born" from tiny embryonic dots which lie in the center of the board. The dots are transformed into aliens, which continually grow in size as they progress to the rim of the board.

1. Flippers. Appear in all boards. The flippers are elusive because they flip between sectors, end over end, as they move toward the rim of the board. When they reach the rim, they continue to flip from sector to sector. The beginning player will be destroyed most frequently by the flippers.

2. Spikers. First appear in board 3. As the spikers move toward the rim, they leave solid lines in their path starting at the center of the board. These lines, called "spikes," explode out of the sector in which they are located at the end of most boards. If the shooter is hit by any one of the spikes, it is destroyed.

3. Tankers. First appear in board 3. Tankers travel in a straightforward path from the center of the board to the rim. However, when they are hit by the player, they are transformed into other types of aliens, as follows:

Cycle 1 and 2 (Boards 3 through 32): Tankers break into two flippers when hit; if they are not hit before they reach the rim of the board, they break into either one or two flippers.

Cycle 3 (boards 33 through 48): Tankers break into either flippers or fuseballs.

Cycle 4 and beyond (board 49 and beyond): Tankers break into either flippers, fuseballs, or pulsars.

4. Fuseballs. First appear in board 11. Fuseballs move back and forth along the edge of each sector. When they reach the rim, they move along it. If they collide with the shooter, they will destroy it. Fuseballs are dangerous, because they cannot be shot when on the rim; they can be Super Zapped, however.

5. Pulsars. First appear in board 17. Pulsars move up and down the board and traverse from sector to sector. They are dangerous because when they pulse in a sector, even if not on the rim, they cause the rim of that sector to disappear. If the shooter happens to be in this sector, he will be destroyed.

Scoring and Number of Shooters

Each of the enemy aliens, when destroyed by the shooter, awards the player varying point values, as shown on the next page.

Alien	Shape	Appears first in board no.	Points when destroyed
Flipper	✕	1	150
Tanker	◈	3	100
Spiker	◉	3	50
Fuseball	🕷	11	250, 500, or 750
Pulsar	⚡	17	200

Bonuses. At the beginning of the game, the player may select one of five levels (or board numbers) at which to begin the game. If he successfully completes the board, he is awarded bonuses, as follows:

Starting board no.	Bonus points for completing board successfully
1	0
3	6,000
5	16,000
7	32,000
9	54,000

If the player hits one of the top eight scores since the machine has been turned on, he may dial in his initials (or some other message) up to three letters, for display on the screen.

At the end of each game, the player is shown his ranking (from 1st to 99th) among all the games played since the machine was turned on.

The player is initially given from two to five shooters, depending upon the machine setting. He is awarded additional shooters for each 20,000 points scored (this number varies from 10,000 to 70,000 in accordance with the settings by machine technicians). There is no limit to the number of additional shooters, but there can be only a maximum of five shooters waiting to be played at any one time. The board turns multi-colored when the player is awarded an additional shooter.

After the completion of a game, the player may continue the next game starting at the highest level he successfully completed. To do this, he is given 30 seconds to push the start button and select the level at which he chooses to start the next game. Bonuses for higher levels are greater than those shown above. For example, the bonus for starting with, and completing, level 13 is 94,000 points; for level 17, the bonus is 154,000 points.

How You Lose

• By colliding with any of the enemy aliens.
• By being hit with the bullets fired by enemy aliens (they are fired only by flippers, tankers, and spikers).
• By being skewered by one of the exploding spikes at the end of a board.

Facts You Should Know

Color. Color is an important way to identify enemy aliens. The color coding of the game is as follows:

Cycle	Boards	Board	Shooter	Flipper	Tanker	Spiker	Pulsar
1	1–16	Blue	Yellow	Orange	Purple	Green	—
2	17–32	Orange-red	Green	Purple	Blue	Light blue	Yellow
3	33–48	Yellow	Blue	Green	Blue	Green	Purple

The fuseballs are multi-colored in all boards.
4th cycle (boards 49–64): The board is light blue.
5th cycle (boards 65–80): The board is invisible. There are no lines defining the board except when the pulsars activate.

6th cycle (boards 81–96): The board is green (again visible).

Boards 97, 98, and 99: The boards, green in color, appear in one of the 16 shapes, selected randomly.

7. Strategies

Selection of Skill Level

You may choose from one of five skill levels (1, 3, 5, 7, or 9) at the beginning of the first game. Since the bonus awards are higher than the scores that can be racked up if the lower levels are completed, you should start the game at the highest level at which you have a high probability of completing the board successfully. This also offers the advanced player the additional advantage of being able to avoid the play of earlier (presumably boringly easy) boards.

Figure 7–4 shows the average scores you will reach if you play without any bonus—that is, starting at level 1—and complete boards 1 through 8 (column A). Columns B, C, and D show the average scores you will reach for the first eight boards if you select skill level 3, 5, and 7, respectively.

Figure 7-4

Average Scores for Completing Boards 1 Through 8 with and without Bonus Awards (in Thousands of Points)

Successful completion through board no.	Start at level 1— NO bonus (A)	Start at level 3— 6,000 bonus (B)	Start at level 5— 16,000 bonus (C)	Start at level 7— 32,000 bonus (D)
1	1½	—	—	—
2	3⅓	—	—	—
3	6–7	9	—	—
4	9	11½–12	—	—
5	13–14	15½	20	—
6	17–18	18½	23	—
7	21	26	27	35
8	24	30–31	31½	40

As you can see, the greater the starting skill level, the higher the scores from completing a given board level. Thus you should try for the highest possible bonus if you feel confident that you can clear the board at that level.

If you choose a skill level at which you have little chance of successfully completing the board, your total score will probably suffer—that is, your score would be higher if you racked up the points from completion of the lower-level boards.

You may prefer to start at level 1, or a level well below your skill, just to play longer. You'll probably sacrifice total score by doing this, but you'll find yourself expending fewer quarters per hour in the arcade.

Completing Levels 1 and 2

These two boards, in which only flippers attack you, are readily completed. Merely fire at the flippers by dialing to the correct sector. Fire as early in the game as possible. This will tend to restrict aliens to the center of the board, an innocuous location. It is when the flippers get to the rim that the shooter is threatened.

A general rule is: When each board first appears, fire blindly and at random. The board will be tiny and the aliens will just be emerging from the tiny dots in the center of the board. But you will destroy some of them early in the game, saving you grief later on during the board.

If you are threatened at any time by a flipper on the rim, hit the Super Zapper button. (It's best to keep the middle finger of your left hand on the FIRE button and your left thumb resting beside the Super Zapper button so you can fire it without looking.) The Super Zapper will clear all existing aliens from the board, although more may subsequently be formed from the little dots in the center.

Each board is completed when all the dots have formed aliens and all the aliens have reached the rim (whether or not they are destroyed).

When you complete board 1, your score should be about 1,500 points. When you complete board 2, your score should be about 3,300 points.

Completing Levels 3 Through 8

The game gets more complicated at level 3 for two reasons:
1. Tankers appear. Tankers are dangerous because when hit, they form two flippers, each of which poses a threat to the player.
2. Spikers appear. Spikers are relatively innocuous, since they usually do not reach the rim of the board and threaten the player. However, spikers create lines or spikes which can destroy the player at the end of the board.

At the end of the board, the message "Avoid Spikes" will be displayed. Move to a sector in which no spike is located. If you don't, the shooter will be destroyed by the spike which explodes out of your sector.

First shoot the tankers and flippers which are closest to the rim. Flip back and forth over several sectors while shooting these targets, because the flippers move from sector to sector and the tankers form flippers which move from sector to sector. Keep the FIRE button depressed continuously and strafe several sectors until the flippers disappear.

If flippers reach the rim, you may destroy them by (1) pushing the Super Zapper button, or (2) waiting in a sector and firing the instant a flipper comes at you from a contiguous sector (it will take a few games to get the timing of this move down perfectly).

During the board, be aware of which sectors have no spikes. Then you can quickly dial to this sector when the "Avoid Spikes" message is flashed.

Completing Level 9 and Beyond

At level 9, spikes develop in every sector of the board. This poses a threat to you, because unless one of the sectors is cleared, you will be hit by a spike at the end of the board.

The best strategy is to select a base sector, preferably one at the extremes of the board (i.e., the sector on the far left or far right), and clear it of spikes. Concentrate on hitting aliens in several adjacent sectors only (ignoring other portions of the board) and keeping the base sector clear.

When flippers approach, shoot them when they're in the sector contiguous to you or Super Zap them. Don't panic if two flippers approach you, one from each side. With proper timing, you can destroy both flippers at the same time—the timing will take some practice.

Since you're trying to destroy nearly everything in sight, you may be drawn to moving toward and shooting at enemy bullets. Avoid this tendency! You get *no* points for shooting an enemy bullet and you risk getting hit by it.

To succeed at TEMPEST, you must move rapidly and accurately from sector to sector. This takes a light, deft touch on the control knob, which is best gripped between the thumb and middle finger, with the index finger resting lightly on the upper side of the knob.

8. MORE BANG FOR YOUR BUCK: CENTIPEDE™

CENTIPEDE is a fast-moving, action-packed game with imaginative sound effects and multi-colored graphics. Its popularity is partly due, no doubt, to the fact that the average player can keep the game going on one quarter for a longer time than is the case with most of the other games.

1. Basic Objective

To score points by shooting various objects on the screen and to stay alive by avoiding contact with any of them.

2. Scenario

You are at the bottom of a vertical field of mushrooms. You have a gun, shaped like the head of a snake, which fires rapidly and can move anywhere in the lower fifth of the field.

Multi-segmented centipedes appear at the top and descend slowly through the mushrooms, row by row. Every few seconds a spider, moving erratically and irregularly, jumps around the bottom portion of the field, threatening you. Periodically fleas dive-bomb at you from the top, leaving fresh mushrooms in their wake. A scorpion also moves across the field; when the centipede hits any mushroom that the scorpion touched, it dives to the bottom of the screen.

If any of the centipede segments or the spider or the fleas collide with your gun, it is destroyed.

3. Novice, Good, and Expert Scores

• Most novices should be able to clear the first board, scoring up to 3,000 points.

• Good players score between 10,000 and 60,000 points.

• Experts score over 100,000 points, reaching 700,000 points and even higher.

4. Controls

Complexity rating: Average.

On the right side of the control board is a track ball, which is rotated to maneuver the gun in any direction. The gun can move anywhere in the lower fifth of the screen, which is called the "player's portion."

Figure 8-1

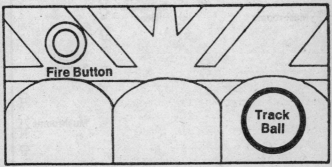

On the left is the FIRE button, which, when depressed, causes the player's gun to shoot upward. Although only one player missile may appear on the screen at one time, the next shot is automatically fired when the previous one is expended, if the button is held down.

Quick movement of the gun and rapid, accurate fire are the keys to success at CENTIPEDE.

5. The Board

The board consists of 30 rows and 30 columns and displays a variety of insects and one vegetable. The dramatis personae:

1. Mushrooms—randomly set around the board.
2. Centipedes—with a head (distinguished by a pair of little eyes) and from 1 to 11 trailing body segments.
3. Spiders—which appear from either side of the screen and jump around the lower one-third of the board.

Figure 8–2

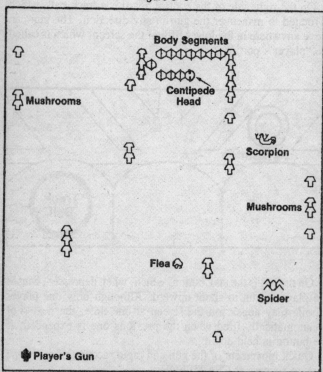

4. Fleas—which appear at the top of the board and dive-bomb to the bottom, leaving mushrooms in their wake.

5. Scorpions—which enter from either side and move across the screen, always staying in the same row.

6. Characteristics

Scoring and Number of Guns

Destroying a mushroom (requires four hits):	1 point
Destroying a centipede body segment:	10 points
Destroying a centipede head:	100 points
Destroying a flea (requires two hits):	200 points
Destroying a spider:	300, 600, or 900 points (the closer the spider to the gun, the more points)
Destroying a scorpion:	1,000 points
Consolation bonus when losing a gun:	5 points for each poisoned mushroom and each partially destroyed mushroom.

The game can be set to give the player from two to five guns; most games are set at three guns. Extra guns are awarded at either 10,000, 12,000, 15,000, or 20,000 points; most games are set at 12,000 points. The player may be awarded an unlimited number of extra guns, except that there can never be more than six guns queued up, waiting to be played.

There are two game-difficulty settings. In the easy game, the spider moves slowly and speeds up when a score of 5,000 points is reached. In the difficult game, the spider speeds up at a score of 1,000 points and moves more erratically than in the easy game.

How You Lose

By colliding with any centipede head or body segment or with a flea or spider.

Facts You Should Know

Centipedes. Centipedes enter the center of the screen at the top row and move across the screen. Whenever they encounter a mushroom, or run into the end of the screen, they change direction and descend one row.

During the first board, there is only one centipede, which consists of a head and 11 body segments. During the second board, the game becomes more challenging, as there are two centipedes, one with a head and 10 body segments, and another with only a head. On the third board, it's even worse: there are three centipedes, one with a head and 9 body segments, and two with only a head. This pattern continues until the 12th board, when 12 separate centipedes with only a head appear.

This cycle repeats starting with the 13th board, except that the centipedes move faster.

If a centipede is hit in the head, the head turns into a mushroom and the next body segment becomes the head. If it's hit in a segment, the segment becomes a mushroom and (unless the hit segment is the tail) the centipede splits into two centipedes, each going in a different direction. The tail of the original centipede becomes the head of the newly formed centipede.

When a centipede (with body segments) reaches the bottom of the screen, its tail is detached and turns into a head. After the centipede traverses one row, it ascends row by row until it reaches the top row of the player's portion. Then it starts descending again, and so on. While this is happening, new heads continually appear from the sides of the player's portion. The longer it takes the player to clear the board, the more frequently are the new heads released (this is the main reason why destruction of the centipede(s) before it reaches the bottom is essential to the average player's survival).

The Spider. The spiders jump erratically and progress across the screen, moving either vertically or at 45-degree angles. Because they move so elusively, they are both dangerous and difficult to destroy.

The spider travels only in the lower one-third or so of the board. It never moves backward—for example, if it enters the screen from the right, it moves only vertically or to the left. never reversing back to the right.

The spider destroys mushrooms it touches (no points are awarded) and also destroys the gun if it collides with it (no points here, either). If the spider makes it across the screen without getting hit, the next spider appears more quickly.

The Flea. Fleas start to appear (with a helpful accompanying dive-bombing sound) during the second board. In early boards, the fleas come out only when there are less than five mushrooms in the player's portion. In later boards, they attack with greater frequency, appearing when a greater number of mushrooms remain in the player's portion.

After they are hit once, the fleas speed up; after they are hit twice, they disappear.

The Scorpion. Scorpions start to appear, with their own unique sound, in the fourth board. Although they move slowly (faster in later boards), it's often difficult to shoot them because they appear high on the board and intervening mushrooms often preclude a direct line of sight to them.

The scorpion "poisons" any mushroom it touches. When the centipede touches a poisoned mushroom, the centipede dives down directly to the bottom of the screen. If its head is shot, however, the centipede resumes its normal snaking pattern.

Later boards. A board is completed after the entire centipede is destroyed. Then the mushrooms and just about everything else turn a new exotic color, and the process begins anew. Naturally, the boards become progressively more difficult. Things really start speeding up at 60,000 points—the spider becomes more elusive and dangerous, and the fleas start diving at an alarming velocity.

7. Strategies

Beginning Strategy

Your first goal should be to clear the first board *before* the centipede reaches the bottom row (it's a lot harder to shoot the centipede when he gets there, and more heads start appearing).

You have quite a bit of time at the beginning, so you can do something else constructive, too—namely, clear the player's portion of the board of mushrooms. This will prevent this centipede (and future ones, if you last long enough to see any) from encountering mushrooms in your zone and descending too rapidly. Here's the strategy:

1. At the very beginning of the game, start firing away at the lower mushrooms. Shoot as fast as you can, get rid of a mushroom (by pumping four shots into it), and move as quickly as you can to the next mushroom. The faster you shoot 'em, the more you'll get.

2. To speed up your shooting, always keep the gun as high (to the north) as possible. This is because the closer you are to the target, the faster the bullets come out. In fact, if you're going to destroy two mushrooms which are in line vertically, move north after getting the lower one until you touch the higher one. They'll disappear a lot faster.

Figure 8–3·

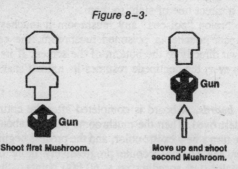

Shoot first Mushroom.   Move up and shoot
                               second Mushroom.

3. Don't hang around either lateral edge of the screen unless you *know* where the spider is. Many beginning players get

zapped at the sides, as the spider enters and miraculously hones in on the exact location of the gun before there's a chance to duck.

4. When the centipede gets about halfway down the screen, start shooting at it. Also destroy the mushrooms it creates when it's hit, so it will come down slower.

5. Try to shoot the spider (he's worth a *lot* of points), but initially do it at a safe distance, settling for the 300 or 600 points. His moves are really tricky, and the beginning player loses more guns to the spider than in any other way. When you get good, you can try to shoot him up close for the 900 points, but that's a dangerous move for a novice.

6. If you're not gunning for the spider, be conservative and stay behind him as much as you can—that is, if he's moving to the left, stay to his right. That way, you'll *never* get hit by him.

7. When you clear the board, don't take a rest. Keep shooting at the lower mushrooms as fast as you can so you'll be in a better position for the next board.

Advanced Strategy

You've got two choices when playing CENTIPEDE—(1) stretching the duration of your game (and your quarter) or (2) going for a lot of points soon. I'd advise starting with the conservative strategy until you're quicker with the controls. Then go for the points. The first strategy requires the following:

1. Stay away from the edges as much as possible (and be ready, if you are at the edge, to roll that track ball *fast* when a spider appears).

2. Shoot spiders only when they're a safe distance from the gun (at least five or more rows away).

3. Shoot fleas only when they're at least one-fifth of the screen above you—certainly no closer.

4. Start on the centipede when it's no more than halfway down the screen.

The more aggressive strategy for points is basically the direct opposite of the previous strategy:

1. Go for the 900 points by waiting until the spider is just about to hit the gun before firing.

2. Pick off many fleas (for the 200 points) even if you zip over to the correct column at the very last minute when the flea is almost at the bottom.

3. Start on the centipede as late as possible to give you more time to hit the point-laden spiders and fleas.

Bottom-row strategy. In later boards, it's inevitable that the centipede will reach the bottom of the screen. When it hits a poison mushroom, for example, it will crash down at you, and your first instinct will be to hide your eyes or run away.

Don't panic! The centipede won't crash into you if you stay in the bottom row—it stops at the second row. In fact, after it traverses the second row, it starts rising *away* from you.

Stay cool. Shoot the centipede, but *stay in the bottom row!* Then pick off heads and body segments just as fast as you can. You're playing a game of catch-up now, trying to pick off the pieces faster than they are created.

Centipede ducking. Alas, on the second descent (after ascending to the top of the player's portion), the centipede does enter the bottom row. This is when the men get separated from the boys. You've got to duck the centipede segments, while firing at them. This requires a high degree of skill—in fact, if and when you master centipede ducking, you're close to joining the ranks of the experts. It requires a hand-eye skill similar to that needed in DEFENDER™ and STARGATE™.

One clue: Watch for segment formations as they traverse the screen and operate the track ball so the gun jumps through the gaps in the formations. Of course, at times there are either tiny gaps or no gaps. All you can do then is brace yourself for the crash.

Fine Points

1. When you get good, be discriminating in the use of your shots. Fire only when you know what you're aiming at. Use only four shots per mushroom. Don't fire blindly and waste

shots. If you do, you risk not having ammunition to save yourself (such as when a flea, which, as you know, must be hit twice, is right on you).

2. Aim for centipede heads, rather than body segments. The centipede won't split off into more irksome sub-centipedes and, of course, you'll get 100 rather than 10 points per segment destroyed.

Advanced techniques. An advanced technique that's really difficult: Try to clear the whole screen of mushrooms at the very beginning of the game. This strategy takes the ultimate economy in allocating shots. It also requires leaving five mushrooms in the player's portion, so fleas don't come down and create more mushrooms. But it's not easy—you've got to duck between the mushrooms you've left intentionally as you shoot at the higher mushrooms. And you've got to—get this—avoid hitting the centipede, because that will create more mushrooms and make the centipede come down on you faster.

(If you feel like fooling around with the game a little, see if you can shoot all the mushrooms out at the beginning, even if you have to sacrifice a few guns. If you lose a gun before the centipede reaches the bottom, the game resets, another centipede starts from the top—and *no* fleas come out! You've got lots more time to keep destroying mushrooms.)

It's awesome to watch advanced boards. The screen is nothing but mushrooms, many of them poisoned. (If a centipede hits an area where there's nothing but mushrooms, it shoots down, vertically.) I saw a game in which the player had 735,800 points and six guns in reserve. The top 14 lines of the screen were about 98% mushrooms.

When you get to this level, there's an expert strategy that can be tried. Let virtually the entire screen fill with mushrooms. Just keep one open vertical lane and keep your gun under it or ready to move under it. Many of the centipede segments will come down that lane. You can zero in on it and zap 'em good!

⑨. A FREE SHOT AT THE ALIENS: GALAGA™

GALAGA is Midway Manufacturing Co.'s sequel to GALAXIAN™. It offers a number of exciting new features that no doubt account for its being the most successful sequel game. GALAGA is unique in its detailed mathematical evaluation of the arcadian's playing efficiency.

1. Basic Objective

To stay alive, by shooting enemy aliens and avoiding collision with them or their missiles.

2. Scenario

You are in a ship, which can move horizontally, and are threatened by flying aliens. Five groups of aliens appear, one by one, from above and from your flanks. They flit around the sky and finally create a formation overhead. Then the aliens peel off and attack, firing missiles as they descend and swerve to avoid your missiles.

The aliens, as in GALAXIAN, can disappear below you and reappear above, either rejoining the formation or continuing their attack.

If you destroy several entire waves, the aliens give you a free shot at them—that is, you may shoot them without their firing back. Your shooting efficiency is then displayed, in bright numerals across the sky for all the world to see.

When your ships are all gone, so is your world.

3. Novice, Good and Expert Scores

• It is not unusual for beginning players to get through the first board—scoring up to 5,000 points—because the five forming groups do *not* fire at the player during the first board.

• Good players score up to 50,000 points.

• Experts score from 100,000 to 600,000 points, and George from the New York City's Fascination Arcade turned the machine over by scoring over 1,000,000 points. (Send me your top scores.)

4. Controls

Complexity rating: Average.

As in GALAXIAN, the player has a two-directional knob for the left hand to move the ship horizontally, and a FIRE button for the right hand, to shoot missiles.

Figure 9-1

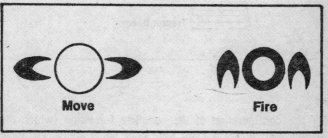

Move   Fire

The Board

The board, with the aliens in formation, is shown in Figure 9-2. The player's ship is at the bottom of the screen. Note the pyramidal structure below the "Boss" Galaga; its purpose is explained later.

Figure 9-2

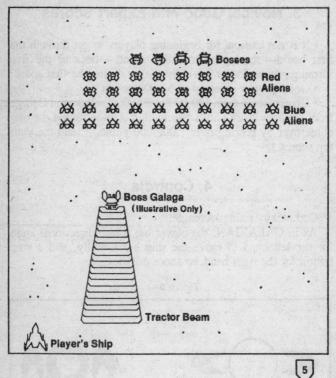

Bosses

Red Aliens

Blue Aliens

Boss Galaga
(Illustrative Only)

Tractor Beam

Player's Ship

5

The configuration of the complete formation (which the player will rarely, if ever, see, since some aliens will have been destroyed prior to their reaching the formation) is as follows:

Top row:	4 bosses
2nd row:	8 red aliens
3rd row:	8 red aliens
4th row:	10 blue aliens
5th row:	10 blue aliens

The number of the board is determined by interpreting little figures that look like military insignia in the lower right-hand portion of the board:

Figure 9–3

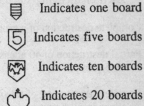

Indicates one board

Indicates five boards

Indicates ten boards

Indicates 20 boards

Thus if 🛡🛡🛡🛡🛡🛡 is shown, the player is on his 19th board.

The players with the five top scores may enter their initials for display on the screen.

6. Characteristics

Scoring and Number of Ships

Points are awarded for shooting aliens, as follows:

Blue aliens:	50 points in formation;	100 while attacking.*
Red aliens:	80 points in formation;	160 while attacking.*
Boss Galaga:†	150 points in formation;	400 points, if alone.*
		800 points, if with 1 escort.
		1,600 points, if with 2 escorts.

*Includes while entering screen in groups.
†Points for hitting bosses not awarded until the second time they are hit. The first time, bosses turn from green to blue.

All three birds:	bonus of 1,000, 1,500, 2,000, or 3,000 points, depending on which stage is being played.

Points for challenging stages:
Each challenging stage consists of five flying groups.

Complete destruction of a group:	bonus of 1,000 (stages 3 and 7), 1,500 and more in later stages.
Partial destruction of 40 aliens in all 5 groups:	bonus of 100 points per alien hit.
Complete destruction of all (40) aliens in all 5 groups:	additional bonus of 10,000 points.

The player is given three ships and awarded extra ships after reaching various point scores. The most common setting is for one additional ship at 20,000 points and one more ship for every 70,000 points thereafter. Extra ship settings are being raised, however, as players get better.

How You Lose

By being hit by any of the aliens or their missiles. Also by having the last ship captured.

Facts You Should Know

Attack stages. There are attack stages and challenging stages (each of which constitutes a "board"), each with its own characteristics.

1. At the beginning of each attack stage, five groups of eight or more aliens fly onto the screen, as follows:

1st group: red and/or blue aliens, from the top of the screen.
2nd group: red and green (the latter, the forebears of the bosses) from the player's flank(s).
3rd group: red and/or blue aliens from the flank(s).

4th group: blue aliens from the top of the screen.
5th group: same as 4th group.

The alien groups fire missiles at the player in all stages except the 1st and 10th stages and several stages thereafter.

2. The aliens which are not destroyed by the player's missiles converge into a formation at the top of the screen. In later stages, some of the aliens in the groups do not fly into the formation, but fly off the bottom of the screen.

The formation moves in unison, both vertically and horizontally. The background of stars and space bodies also moves, which exaggerates the movement of the formation. Despite this, the aliens in formation are easier to pick off in formation than in GALAXIAN.

3. The aliens peel off and attack the ship, firing missiles as they descend.

Bird trios. Periodically, one of the blue aliens in formation metamorphosizes into a trio of swarming birds, which attack the ship. The player is given both an audio and visual warning of this event; sounds emanate which remind one of the oboe duck sound in *Peter and the Wolf* and the blue alien turns color and flashes (too briefly to be of much help to the average player).

This trio is notable because the player receives a healthy bonus for destroying all three birds. The trailing bird makes a loop, and, if it is not shot before it flies off the bottom of the screen (and the other two birds are), it rematerializes at the top.

Captured ships. A boss, either green or blue, will periodically swoop down and send out a pyramid-shaped blue "tractor beam" (see Figure 9–2). If the ship is caught at the base of this beam, it is "captured." It swirls into the field and the boss takes off with the kidnapped ship, which turns red.

The captured ship then flies in tandem with the abducting boss. If that boss is hit (while attacking only), the captured ship returns to the ground and links to the ship being maneuvered by the player. Be careful here; it's possible to shoot your own ship, a senseless—indeed gross—waste of resources.

The player now has two ships in tandem firing at the aliens, which offers two advantages:

• Double firepower. A single ship may have only two missiles on the screen at one time; with a double ship, the limit now becomes four.

• The player can cover a wider range of the screen with his shots.

Of course, the trade-off is that the two ships offer a much wider target for the aliens and their missiles and are more difficult to protect. As we will see, there are times when it is preferable for the player to have a ship captured intentionally.

Challenging stages. After the first two attack stages, and after every subsequent three attack stages, there is a challenging stage.

These are fun because the player cannot lose his ship during them and because the aliens fly in often-predictable patterns which allow the player to pick them off, one by one, with rapid fire—if he does it right.

The challenging stages also have five groups of entering aliens:

1. A group of eight aliens from the top.
2. A group of eight aliens from the flank(s).
3. A second group of eight aliens from the flank(s).
4. A group of eight aliens from the top.
5. A second group of eight aliens from the top.

The challenging stages are a key to high scoring at GALAGA because of the hefty bonus awards described earlier. At the end of each challenging stage, the screen displays the number of aliens you destroyed—there are a total of 40. If you shot 40 out of 40, an ego-flattering PERFECT message flashes on the screen (no, if you miss them all, it doesn't print KLUTZ).

7. Strategies

Beginning Strategy

First concentrate on getting through the first stage. The best way to do this is to learn where the five groups of aliens come from and know the best position for the ship to shoot each of the groups. These are shown below:

Figure 9–4

1st Group
4 red and 4 blue aliens come on to the screen from the top.

2nd Group
4 red and 4 green aliens enter from the left.

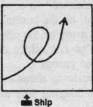

3rd Group
8 red aliens enter from the right.

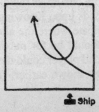

4th Group
8 blue aliens enter from the top.

5th Group
8 blue aliens enter from the top.

Fire rapidly at the aliens, hitting the FIRE button twice rapidly (to release your maximum of two missiles). As soon as the first missile is expended, hit the button again—twice.

You should destroy many of the aliens before they get to the formation—and at no risk, since during this board they don't fire at you when in groups.

Then pick off the remaining aliens in the formation—or as they attack you—while dodging their missiles.

Advanced Strategy

Unless you're a highly dexterous rapid-fire improviser, success at GALAGA depends upon Knowing the Enemy. During each stage, try to anticipate where the aliens are coming from and where your ship should be for maximum destructive results. The really dedicated player could develop a strategy such as the stage-one strategy shown earlier, for every stage.

Letting a ship be captured. Once you become fairly proficient at shooting, a good strategy is to let your ship (assuming, of course, that it's not the last one) be captured during the stages immediately preceding each challenging stage (i.e., stages 2, 6, 10, 14, 18, 22, 26, etc.). This is because you'll have more firepower during the challenging stages—and not have to worry about your double-ship getting hit. Remember, the enemy does not fire during those stages.

You'll have a much better chance of getting the group bonuses and may even earn the perfect-score bonus of 10,000 points.

In the first two challenging stages (3 and 7), the average shooter should be able to get a perfect score by keeping the double-ship in the center of the board and firing rapidly and accurately. In later stages, when the aliens start to move more evasively, the ship(s) must be maneuvered with skill. For example, in stage 27, the aliens evade abruptly, swerving at both right angles and 45-degree angles.

Here's a tip for recapturing your ship. Notice how the boss and your captured ship move. They often loop, either clockwise or counterclockwise, while descending. If the former, the unit will reach the bottom of the screen on the left side; if the latter, on the right side (Figure 9–5). You should try to be at precisely those locations so you can pick off the boss and regain your ship.

Figure 9–5

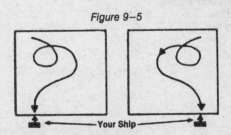

Your Ship

Other tips. If bosses come down with escorts, don't worry about destroying the escorts first. The 800 and 1,600 boss point values are awarded when you destroy the boss, irrespective of whether the escorts are hit or not.

When the groups enter the screen in the early stages, their missiles tend to be located toward the center of the screen. Stay on the sides until the missiles pass by; then move around freely as necessary to destroy aliens.

Shooting Accuracy

At the end of each game, the screen prints the following information:

Number of Shots Fired	XXX
Number of Hits	XXX
Hit-Miss Ratio	XX %

The hit-miss ratio is a misnomer; what is shown is percentage of successful shots.

Good players generally fire between 55% and 70% of their shots accurately. Chances are if you're scoring below 50%, you should sharpen up your accuracy by better anticipating where the aliens will be.

One player who scored only 14,000 points hit on 39.7% of his shots. Another scored 338,000 points, fired a total of 2,563 shots, and hit on 1,715, or 66.9% of them.

Remember though, the name of the game is not Percent Hits—it's Total Points.

10. WORSE THAN PILOTING A 747: STARGATE™

STARGATE, Williams Electronics, Inc.'s sequel to DE-FENDER™, is the most difficult video game in existence to-day. Its controls are even more complicated than those of its predecessor.

You will save *many* quarters by first practicing on and becoming adroit at DEFENDER before trying to cope with STARGATE.

1. Basic Objective

As in DEFENDER, to stay alive as long as possible, pref-erably long enough to be awarded extra ships so you can stay continually ahead of the game.

2. Scenario

The story line is essentially identical to that of DEFENDER. You are protecting men (now called humanoids, but we shall continue to call them men) from kidnapping by enemy landers.

There are significant complicating differences:

• There are far more types of enemy aliens, with different shapes, colors, and movement characteristics.

• The planet disappears after every fifth wave whether you've lost all the men or not.

• Periodically your ship is subject to a "Yllabian Dogfight" in which you are pitted against many (get this) Yllabian Space Guppies and other aliens. As you will find out, Yllabian Space Guppies and their missiles are no pushovers.

• You must also survive a "Firebomber Showdown" periodically—an even more challenging test of your aerial skill.

3. Novice, Good, and Expert Scores

• The novice game goes so quickly it's absurd. I saw someone score only 225 points yesterday after three almost instantaneous crashes.

• The good player (equivalent to the excellent DEFENDER player) can score up to 30,000 or 40,000 points.

• The expert player can score hundreds of thousands of points. But these guys are not only fabulously coordinated, they're rare.

4. Controls

Complexity rating: Highest.

The controls are identical to DEFENDER, with a seventh button thrown in:

The left hand operates a two-directional joystick (for vertical ship movement) and a REVERSE button.

In the center is the HYPERSPACE button.

The right hand operates FIRE, THRUST, and SMART BOMB buttons, as in DEFENDER. You must also somehow control a fourth button, the INVISO button, with this hand.

Figure 10-1

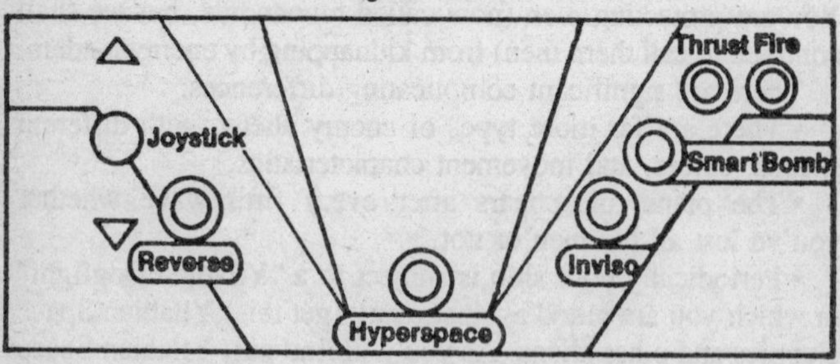

5. The Board

Once again, identical to DEFENDER, except that:

• New aliens of strange shapes, sizes and proclivities appear both on the screen and on the scanner.

• The amount of Inviso time remaining is shown as a red line, below the section of each player's scoring box that shows the number of smart bombs remaining.

Figure 10-2

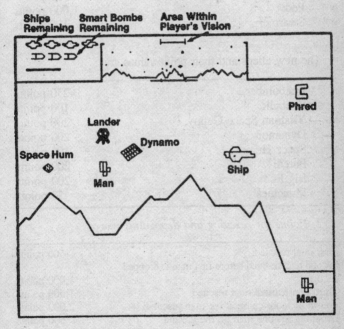

6. Characteristics

Scoring and Number of Ships

1. Points for blasting aliens

Points awarded for blasting the DEFENDER aliens are unchanged.

Lander:	150 points
Mutant:	150 points
Baiter:	200 points
Bomber:	250 points
Pod:	1,000 points
Swarmer:	150 points

The new aliens and their point values are:

Firebomber:	250 points
Fireball:	100 points
Yllabian Space Guppy:	200 points
Dynamo:	200 points
Space Hum:	100 points
Phred:	200 points
Big Red:	200 points
Munchies:	50 points

2. Points for rescuing and depositing men

First man rescued:	500 points
Second man rescued before first man is dropped off:	1,000 points
Third consecutive man rescued:	1,500 points
Fourth or more consecutive man rescued:	2,000 points
Dropping off one man on the ground:	500 points
Dropping off more than one man on the ground:	500 points for each man dropped
Man landing safely on the ground all by himself (only possible if he is freed from the lander about an inch or less above the ground):	250 points

3. Bonus for completing waves

A certain number of bonus points is given for each man remaining; multiply the figures below by the number of men remaining:

Wave 1:	100 points
Wave 2:	200 points
Wave 3:	300 points
Wave 4:	400 points
Wave 5 and beyond:	500 points

4. Consolation Award

25 points when the ship crashes.

5. The Stargate Warp

This is a key feature of STARGATE. If you are carrying four or more men and enter the STARGATE (the rectangular box that floats around the sky) you will warp ahead three waves (until wave 10)! This is highly desirable because:

• You get a bonus of 2,000 points for every man remaining.

• You get closer to the next bonus wave, when new men and a new planet are awarded.

• Your huge bonus gets you closer to awards of extra ships, smart bombs, and more Inviso.

If you go into the STARGATE with less then four men, no warp takes place. You will either be relocated at the spot where a lander is kidnapping one of the men or, if there are none, you will be immediately transported to the opposite side of the planet.

New ships, new men, and new planets. (What else is there in life?) The player is given a new set of men and a new planet after every five waves (that is, at the beginning of waves 6, 11, 16, 21, etc.). The player is awarded an extra ship, an extra smart bomb, and more Inviso time after scoring a certain number of points; 10,000 points is currently the most prevalent setting for these awards.

If the player inserts one quarter at the beginning of a game, he gets 3 ships, 3 smart bombs, and 3 "units" of Inviso.

If he inserts two quarters at the beginning, he gets 7 ships, 7 smart bombs, and 7 units of Inviso.

How You Lose

I can blithely say, only one way—by being hit by any of the aliens or their missiles. However, it usually seems that there's an infinite number of these around.

Facts You Should Know

Ego facts. STARGATE, more than most games, caters to the player's ego.

1. When you are qualified to be listed as one of the top scorers on the screen, the machine displays the following ego-inflating message: "You have entered the realm of the STAR-GATE Immortals."

2. The "all-time" top scorer is displayed in huge letters across the top of the screen. He is given 20 spaces for his name, message, phone number or obscene saying, plus three letters for his initials.

3. The next 39 all-time scorers (the "immortals") are displayed, with the standard 3 letters allowed.

4. The six daily high scorers ("the mortals") are shown.

If the HYPERSPACE button is pushed, the ego display is shown on the screen (you could sort of inadvertently hit the button with your elbow as you and your girlfriend walked by the machine).

The game records scores of up to seven digits, or to put it in arcade player parlance, "It turns over at 9,999,975, man."

"Secrets"

If you push the REVERSE button while the game is not in play, some "secrets" of the game are displayed on the screen. The secrets revealed by the manufacturer, far from all of them, are:

1. An explanation of the STARGATE Warp. You must fly forward into the STARGATE, not backward.

2. While using Inviso, your ship is invisible (and thus immune to destruction) and yet you still destroy everything in your path.

3. When the ship enters the STARGATE, it will transport you to a portion of the planet where men are being kidnapped. If there are none of these, you rematerialize on the opposite side of the planet.

4. As in DEFENDER, the planet disappears when all men are lost. (Survival then becomes exceedingly difficult.)

5. A smart bomb destroys all aliens on the screen at the time it is released (we knew this secret from DEFENDER).

Other Secrets

Know Your Enemy:

Alien*	Shape	Color	Points when shot
Firebomber		Multi-colored; spins	250
Fireball		Red and yellow; flashing	100
Yllabian Space Guppy		White, pink, purple, and blue	200
Dynamo		Red and white checks; flashes.	200
Space Hum		Red and white, like baby dynamos.	100
Phred		Purple and white; mouths move like square PAC-MAN.	200
Big Red		Same as phreds, but red and yellow	200
Munchies		All green; look like baby Phreds or Big Reds	50

*New aliens only. For others, see DEFENDER chapter.

Characteristics of New Aliens

Firebombers. They stay in one place (horizontally) on the screen, but move up and down vertically, not very rapidly. After the first wave, they shoot Fireballs to block the player's missiles.

Fireballs. These are the missiles of the Firebombers.

Yllabian Space Guppy. They resemble guppies because they have gill-like middles which "breathe," getting smaller and bigger. They shoot long, skinny white needles, which are lethal, of course.

Dynamo. Dangerous because they fire Space Hums at the ship.

Space Hums. These track the ship wherever it goes and must be shot.

Phreds and Big Reds. Of the "square PAC-MAN®" family, these two come out first. Out of them come Munchies.

Munchies. They are like the babies of Phreds and Big Reds; in fact, they cry when they first appear.

Yllabian Dogfight

This challenge occurs in waves 5, 15, 25, 35, etc. The player battles Yllabian Space Guppies primarily, but a few Dynamos and Swarmers are thrown in for good measure. There's no planet during these waves.

The player gets a 2,500-point bonus for completing the dogfight successfully.

Firebomber Showdown

This occurs in waves 10, 20, 30, 40, etc. The player encounters Firebombers and six Pods. There is no bonus for completing this.

"Pod Intersection"

There's a pod intersection indicator at the base of the scanner. This is a timing countdown device that lets you know when Pods come together. It occurs during regular waves and during the Firebomber Showdowns (not during the Yllabian Dogfight because there are no Pods then).

Inviso Button

The button must be held down for the ship to remain in the Inviso state. The indicator in the score box tells how much Inviso (called an "anti-matter cloaking device") remains.

7. Strategies

Wave 1 Strategy

During wave 1, search out the Landers and rescue men. If you've got one or two men attached to the ship and see a Lander kidnapping another man, go into the STARGATE, reappear where the kidnapping is taking place, destroy the Lander, and collect another man. Keep doing this until you're carrying at least four men.

Then go into the STARGATE and warp ahead three waves.

Some players try to pick up all 10 men before going into the STARGATE. This way they get 2,000 points for every pickup beyond the third man. This can be accomplished with practice, because the Landers move much more slowly during wave 1.

Shooting Aliens

Firebombers and Fireballs. Since Firebombers move up and down and fire Fireballs to block your bullets, it's best to get above the Firebombers and then descend, firing steadily as you do, so the Firebombers can't elude you. It's necessary to really spray them to overcome the Fireballs they'll fire to block your shots.

Yllabian Space Guppies. They're tricky to shoot because they fire the long needles at the ship. But the needles can be dodged by staying in front of them.

Dynamos and Space Hums. Don't get close to Dynamos; shoot them from a safe distance before they have a chance to fire Space Hums at you. The Space Hums follow the ship wherever it goes, so they must be destroyed.

Phreds, Big Reds, and Munchies. Shoot the parent Phreds and Big Reds quickly before they have a chance to send out Munchies.

The Dogfight

While not as difficult as the Showdown, the big challenge of the Dogfight is the many needles that the Guppies fire. Use Inviso to get out of trouble, especially when in a swarm of Guppies and their needles.

The Showdown

This battle is difficult because there are many Firebombers and they block the player's shots with Fireballs. It's best to clear the screen out with smart bombs. The player can usually win the showdown using three smart bombs, as follows:

1. Watch the pod intersection until it gets to a zero. The Pods should then be congregated on the screen. Fire a smart bomb—for lots of points.
2. Thrust forward a few inches. You'll spot 9 or 10 Firebombers. Blast them all with another smart bomb.
3. There'll be three or four stragglers, which you can spot by looking on the scanner. Thrust up to them and smart-bomb them.

Mission accomplished! You've used three smart bombs, but not lost any ships.

A Final Note

High scores are a lot tougher in STARGATE, because unlike DEFENDER, where the difficulty level tends to flatten out around the 19th wave or so, STARGATE keeps getting harder, as aliens move continually faster and dodge more artfully, as if they're getting smarter.

A friend of mine, Steve Thornock of Las Vegas, plays STARGATE incessantly. In his high game to date he scored 697,000 points and played to wave 45.

Question: Why is the message across the top of *every* STARGATE game in Las Vegas, as of this writing, "The Beatles Forever"?

Clue: One of Steve's favorite songs is "Yesterday."

11. ELECTRONIC GEOMETRY: QIX™

QIX, pronounced "kicks," is a unique game which poses perplexing geometric challenges. It is particularly popular at the several college arcades that I visited across the country.

1. Basic Objective

To partition off as much of the screen as possible with a marker, while preventing the lines of the incompleted segment from being struck by a lightning-shaped QIX (also called a "helix") or other objects.

2. Scenario

A multi-faceted lightning bolt, the QIX, dances around the screen erratically. You must partition off areas of the screen without getting hit by the QIX or by little electronic zappers ("Sparx") that travel along the outside of the screen and along the lines you have drawn (the "Stix"). If you delay, or draw yourself into a corner, you can get zapped by "Fuses" which travel along the path you have drawn.

3. Novice, Good, and Expert Scores

• The novice will have difficulty clearing the first board and scoring beyond 6,000 points.
• The good player can generally get through two or more boards, scoring from 15,000 to 30,000 points.
• Experts score up to 100,000 points and even higher.
These scores are all based on a 75% difficulty-level board

completion setting; there can be wide variations in scores depending upon this setting.

4. Controls

Complexity rating: Average.

A four-directional joystick is located on the left of the control board. This moves the marker in one of four directions: up, down, to the right, or to the left.

Figure 11–1

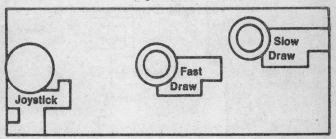

On the right are two buttons, a slow-draw button and a fast-draw button, which set the marker into motion at one of two speeds.

As in DONKEY KONG®, I find it *much* easier to cross hands and operate the joystick with my right hand and the draw buttons with the left. I notice quite a few right-handed players do this, too. Try it; it may help.

5. The Board

The player's marker is designated by a red diamond. Areas partitioned off by the player are shown in color, either blue (if the fast-draw button was used) or yellow (if the slow-draw button was used).

The Sparx, which chase and can destroy the player's marker,

are small objects made up of several red and yellow dots.

The Fuse, which is yellow, appears when the player hesitates in drawing—that is, allows the marker to remain stationary, even if for an instant. The Fuse travels toward the marker down the lines being made by the player, the Stix. If either the Sparx or the Fuse reaches the marker, the marker is destroyed.

The percentage of the screen partitioned off by the player is continually displayed at the top of the screen.

Figure 11-2

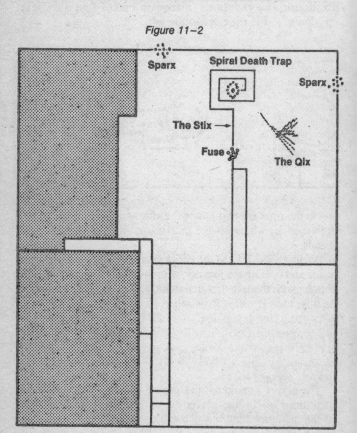

6. Characteristics

Scoring and Number of Markers

Partitioning a segment of the board:	Points are awarded, depending upon the size of the area enclosed by the partition (double points are awarded if the slow-draw button is used, rather than the fast-draw button).
Partitioning off more than (usually) 75% of the screen:	1,000 points per percentage point in excess of 75% (e.g., if 82% of the screen is partitioned off, the player is awarded a bonus of 7, 000 points).
Separating two QIX:	
First time:	Double bonus points
Second time:	Triple bonus points
Third time:	4 × bonus points, etc.

The player gets three markers. No extra markers are awarded.

How You Lose

When the player's marker is struck by a QIX, the Sparx, or a Fuse. If the player partitions off 75% or more of the board, the board has been successfully completed, the bonus (if any) is awarded, and a new board appears.

The percentage criterion can be set at any number from 0% to 99% of the screen. Some arcades have this set at as low as 25%, which increases both the duration of playing time and players' average scores.

Facts You Should Know

1. At the beginning of the first board, there are two Sparx that chase the marker. The Sparx start at the top of the board,

and the marker is formed at the bottom of the board.

2. There is a thin red line, the "Time Line," at the top of the board, which gradually decreases in length from both ends. When the line totally disappears—that is, when the two ends of the line meet—additional Sparx are released. The machine can be adjusted for the time it takes the ends of the Time Line to meet, from 0 to 99 seconds. The most commonly used time is 37 seconds, the factory setting.

When an alarm goes off (sounds like a blaring horn), the Sparx turn blue and become more aggressive in chasing the marker.

3. After the player has begun drawing, if he lets up on the draw button for even a fraction of a second, a Fuse is ignited, which begins chasing the marker. If the player puts the joystick in neutral, making the marker stationary, the Fuse is also ignited. If the player completes an area before the Fuse reaches the marker, he is safe.

4. If the player draws himself into a corner so that he is unable to complete an area, he will be destroyed by the Fuse. This is called the "spiral death trap" because a common way for the player to be trapped is to create a series of quasi-spiral-shaped concentric figures (as shown in Figure 11-2).

5. Many players don't realize that if the joystick is depressed and the draw buttons are not, the marker will travel along the borders of the figures already drawn on the screen. This is an essential technique to position the marker in a safe, desirable location.

6. The first two boards have one QIX. In most games, the second board is set to have the QIX move more aggressively during the second board. In the third and fourth boards, there are two QIX. (The game has four difficulty settings which determine how unpredictably and erratically the QIX move.)

7. Strategies

Beginning Strategy

1. The beginning player should play it safe and use only

the fast-draw button until he gets accustomed to the controls and the velocity of QIX movements.

2. Avoid the natural tendency to start drawing as soon as the marker is formed. Wait for a while; the QIX will often move a safe distance away. At the beginning of the first board, there's usually plenty of time, as the Sparx start on the side of the board opposite from the location where the marker is initially formed.

. 3. Initially, don't take chances. Just partition off small areas, enclosing them rapidly. Be patient and grind away, trying to get your percentage up to 75%; the percentage is continually displayed at the top of the screen.

Advanced Strategy

One effective strategy for more points is to partition off the board in small vertical segments. If the partitions are created such that the segments are quite close to the opposite side of the screen, the movement of the QIX can be severely restricted (see Figure 11–3). The player can then finish the board with a slow draw, getting double points for the huge orange area which is then created.

Figure 11–3

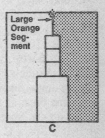

If you start with the fast draw and convert in mid-draw to slow draw, the resulting area will still be blue, not orange, yielding normal (not double) points. Thus there is no reason to do this.

If you start with the slow draw and convert to the fast draw, the resulting area will also be blue. There may be times when it is advisable to do this, such as when the QIX is getting close to your line and you want to enclose the area as quickly as possible.

In boards 1 and 2, try to enclose about 73% to 74% of the board. Then position the marker so a large area may be partitioned off. Remember, you get 1,000 points for every percentage point past 75% of the board that is enclosed. So if your final chunk is (say) 15% of the board (and you started at 74%), you will have enclosed 89% of the board, for a 14,000-point bonus.

Starting with the third board, two QIX appear. Try to separate the QIX from each other, rather than restricting both to the same portion of the board. This can be accomplished by carving out *small* segments down the middle of the board.

If you succeed in separating the QIX in the third board, you'll get double scores for enclosing areas in the fourth board. If you separate the QIX in the fourth board, you'll get triple scores for enclosing areas in the fifth board. Beyond the fifth board, most players go for completion of the required percentage of the board, rather than trying to separate the QIX, which becomes very difficult.

You can sense when you progress from an average player to a good player in QIX. The key: almost superhuman patience. It's really tempting to try to make those long runs up the screen, blocking off huge areas. But don't do it!

Block off tiny areas, one at a time. You know you've arrived, QIX-wise, when you use the joystick a lot, but not the buttons. Without drawing, skirt around the segments you've already drawn and watch where the QIX is going. When you've got some breathing room, quickly bite off a tiny area.

If you see Sparx, all you've got to do is put them behind you. If a Sparx is moving, say, north, stay above it, venture (safely) out to the undrawn area, wait for the Sparx to pass, and return, south of the Sparx. You won't have to worry about that Sparx for a long, long time—it's got to go around the whole screen. Do the same with the other Sparx. If you do, you can forget about the Sparx for a while and concentrate solely on avoiding the QIX and drawing your areas.

It's great when you get QIX confined to a tiny area—sort of like having a tiger in a tank, or a bull in a china closet. When you are ready to enclose the pattern you've been working toward, wait until you're safe from the QIX and the Sparx. Then press the slow-draw button and draw the (you hope) quarter-inch or shorter line to finish the geometric connection. Whappo! The board's maybe 92% complete—and all orange—for lots of points . . . and look at the bonus!

8. Other Versions

QIX II®. Similar to QIX except that a free play is awarded for enclosing more than 90% of the board.

12. FROGS, HIGHWAYS, AND CROCODILES: FROGGER™

FROGGER is a colorful game which is reminiscent of the old Jonathan Winters skit about the frog trying to get across the highway. In the case of FROGGER, however, the poor frog must traverse several lanes of vehicles and also cross a river. The game is particularly pleasant to play because it provides a background of light, mellow music.

1. Basic Objective

To maneuver a series of frogs across a highway and river and steer them safely into "homes" or docks on the other side of the river.

2. Scenario

You're a simple little frog, just trying to make it in a complex world. You've got to cross a highway, avoiding cars in the slow lane, followed by lanes of tractors, dune buggies, more cars, and finally large trucks or "semis."

Then you reach a "base" where you're safe. But now it's time to cross a river which also has "lanes" consisting of turtles, logs, and even crocodiles. Then you've got to jump into your dock or "home."

If you get hit by any of the vehicles, you're a goner. If you jump into the water, it's also all over. Snakes and otters also lurk about trying to gobble you up. Worse yet, you have only 60 "beats" of time to get safely home.

Ah, the life of a frog!

3. Novice, Good, and Expert Scores

• Beginning players may get wiped out after only around 500 to 1,000 points.

• Good players, who can complete several boards, score 5,000 to 15,000 points.

• Expert players reach scores of 70,000 and higher.

4. Controls

Complexity rating: Low.

FROGGER has one quite simple control—a four-directional joystick which moves the frog forward or back and to either side. The joystick must be pushed for each movement of the frog—that is, the frog does not keep jumping if the knob is held in one of the positions continuously.

Figure 12-1

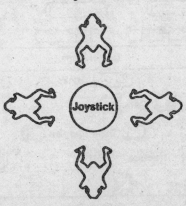

5. The Board

The board consists of a starting base at the bottom, five lanes of vehicles, another base in the center of the screen, and five lanes of turtles, logs, and crocodiles, floating down the river.

At the top of the screen are five docks or homes into which the frog must jump.

Periodically appearing on the second base, and around the river, are snakes, which will destroy the frog if they reach him. Also, swimming in the river are otters, which try to eat the frog as he sits on one of the logs.

Figure 12–2

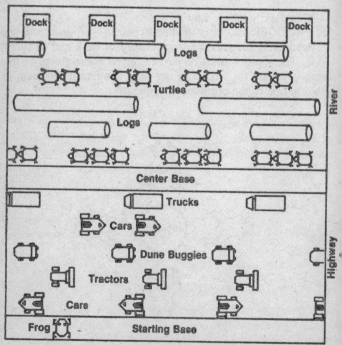

But there's some good news, too. There's a lady frog, dressed in pink, naturally, who periodically appears. If our frog jumps on the lady, or vice versa, and carries her home safely with him, a point bonus is awarded. Further, if the frog lands on a fly when he jumps into a dock, the player gets more points. Sometimes, however, a crocodile will lurk in the dock. If the frog jumps in when it's there, it's instant death.

Each jump of the frog, forward or back, moves the frog one lane. While it's of no particular moment—to game strategy or anything else—the frog may also jump back from the starting base into the row where the timer is located. Unless the player gets a lift out of building a psychological (but not physical) momentum while approaching the first lane, I can see absolutely no reason for this move.

6. Characteristics

Scoring and Number of Frogs

Moving the frog forward one jump:	10 points
Maneuvering a frog safely into a dock:	50 points
For every beat remaining on the timer when a frog reaches a dock:	10 points
Carrying a lady frog to the dock:	200 points
Jumping on a fly in the dock:	200 points
Completing a board, by getting all 5 frogs safely into the 5 docks:	1,000 points

Players are given three, five, or seven frogs, depending on the game setting. An extra frog is usually awarded at 20,000 points. The scores of the top five players are displayed on the screen with their initials.

How You Lose

There are probably more ways to lose in FROGGER than in any other video game:

1. Getting hit by anything on the highway.

2. Jumping into the river.
3. Getting eaten by snakes or otters.
4. Jumping on a diving turtle and not getting off it in time.
5. Floating off the edge of the screen (while on top of logs, turtles, or crocodiles).
6. Jumping into the mouth of a floating crocodile.
7. Missing the dock when trying to jump into it.
8. Jumping into a crocodile in the dock (but not if the crocodile is only halfway into the dock).
9. Jumping into a dock already occupied by a frog.
10. Running out of time before reaching the dock.

Facts You Should Know

Timing bar. The timing bar at the lower right portion of the screen is set to allow the frog 60 beats to get to the dock. It gradually decreases in length as time is used up. When there are only 10 beats left, the timing bar warns the player by turning red.

Turtles. A frog is safe on the back of a red turtle. However, he may remain only briefly on the back of a green turtle. Most turtles stay red continually. One set of turtles in each of the two rows of turtles turns green. They go from red (regular size), to green (regular size), to green (small size). Then there's a hesitation and they change shape in the opposite way—from green (small size), to green (regular size), to red (regular size). If a frog is on the turtle when it is green (small size), it will drown.

Board configuration. The boards get progressively more difficult to complete, as follows:

1st board: Contains one slowly moving car in the 4th lane from the bottom. If the player takes too long to complete the board, the car speeds up and the turtles start moving faster.

2nd board: Two slow cars in the 4th lane.

3rd board: Two fast cars—spread out and thus more dangerous—in the 4th lane.

4th board: Three fast cars in the 4th lane.

5th board: Four fast cars in the 4th lane.

Starting with the 6th board, and every 6th board thereafter, the cycle repeats, except that other complicating factors are introduced. For example, in the 6th board, there is once again only one slow car in the 4th lane, but there are two serpents (one on the center base and one on the logs) and fewer logs in the river.

For the 7th through 11th boards, the number of cars in the fast lane increases once again, and the cycle repeats again at board 12.

The board being played is indicated by little frogs in the lower right corner of the board.

7. Strategies

Beginning Strategy

1. Don't start moving the frog forward as soon as the game starts. Wait for an opening and jump forward when an opening occurs. Or, jump sideways; this saves you time, since rather than waiting for an opening you are jumping toward one.

2. If the frog brushes only lightly against any vehicle, it is destroyed. Be conservative and leave a full space between the frog and the vehicles when crossing the highway.

3. To get through the first board or two, don't worry about time. Most beginning players lose their frogs to highway vehicles or to the river—not to the timer. In early boards, it's not necessary to rush to the dock by narrowly avoiding oncoming vehicles or by taking chances on the river. Large gaps will develop if you're patient enough, and 60 beats is more than enough time to reach the docks in the early boards.

4. Notice that the lady frog always appears on the short logs floating in the 2nd row in the river. If you jump onto the log beside her, you may either move over one or more jumps toward her, or you may wait; she moves around and may jump on you. If the lady appears across the board from you, it's generally not worth wasting time going for her. The main objective is getting to the dock safely and rapidly.

If you're carrying a lady frog and jump into a dock where there is a fly, you get a total of 400 bonus points, 200 for the lady frog and 200 for the fly.

5. The most difficult dock to fill is the one at the extreme left of the board. This is because the frog must be maneuvered so it is to the left of this dock before jumping into it. Observe the timing and spacing of the last line of logs (or, in later boards, of the crocodile). You must ride on a turtle in the 2nd row from the top, moving to the left, and then jump onto a log (or crocodile) before running into the edge of the screen. If you misjudge, and suddenly realize that no log will appear, jump backward onto a right-moving log to avoid crashing into the edge of the screen.

6. It's quite important to become familiar with which group of turtles in each row turns green. To the extent possible, try to keep a mental note at all times of which group turns. Avoid turtles which turn green. It will be a rare emergency when you will have to resort to jumping on a green turtle.

Advanced Strategy

Later boards. The most difficult lane to cross in advanced boards is the 4th lane, which has many fast-moving cars. Timing is the key to getting past this lane. Notice that the fast cars are usually grouped together. Become familiar with the timing of the cars, and navigate the frog so that it crosses this lane in the gaps between the groups of fast cars.

The 11th board is really difficult—there are four fast cars and waiting for you on the center base are two snakes.

Don't forget (as many players do) that you can elude danger by jumping backward. For example, if you're threatened by a snake on a log, jump back to a safe red turtle.

FROGGER takes much concentration—an awareness of where the objects are at all times. Don't lose your frog by inadvertently having him jump forward several times in a row—a natural tendency. I've seen dozens of frogs lost because of this.

As in basketball and marriage, it's best in FROGGER to *think before you leap!*

13. THE FISH THAT WON'T BITE: MAKE TRAX™

MAKE TRAX is a maze-type game which reminds one of PAC-MAN™, except that the two fish that plague the player are a lot smarter than PAC-MAN's four monsters. The game is particularly infuriating because when the player is caught the fish continue to wag their tails happily and a tune (which sounds derisive to me, but I might be paranoid) is played.

1. Basic Objective

• To completely "paint" the maze, avoiding the two chasing fish, and successfully complete as many boards as possible.

• To catch one of six characters who emerge from their "homes" during the board and to clean up the "trax" they leave on the freshly painted paths.

2. Scenario

The player is represented by (get this) a paintbrush, which paints a maze, while being chased by two fish. Periodically other objects come onto the maze and dirty the area already painted. Yes, those areas must be repainted.

3. Novice, Good, and Expert Scores

• Beginning players who do not clear the first board will score up to about 5,000 points.

• Good players, who clear two to four boards, will score from 10,000 to 25,000 points.

• Expert players score up to 300,000 points. As in PAC-MAN, these players use predetermined patterns of movement to clear the boards.

4. Controls

Complexity rating: Low.

The player has only a four-directional joystick stick, which he uses to maneuver the paintbrush around the board.

Figure 13–1

As in most games, it is best to use a light touch in gripping the joystick. Most players hold the joystick between the thumb and the index and middle fingers.

5. The Board

The board is a fairly complex maze, created by dividers, the "homes" of the characters who appear on the board, and the two boxes (the "aquarium") where the fish begin the game. Other features of the board include:

• Six tunnels, one at the top, one at the bottom, and two at each side. When the player enters a tunnel (and does not reverse direction), he emerges from the tunnel which is on the opposite side of the board.

• Two overpasses. At one end of each is a "roller." If the player engages the roller and rolls over a fish, the fish returns to the aquarium (similar to eating a blue monster in PAC-MAN).

Figure 13–2

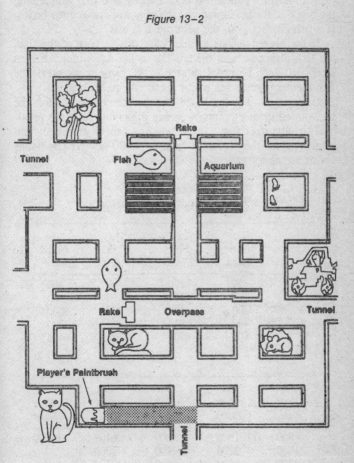

6. Characteristics

The player's paintbrush is chased by two fish which enter the board at the beginning of each play from two center boxes. If a fish catches you, the paintbrush is lost.

If the player pushes a roller over one or both of the fish, the fish disappear and materialize in the aquarium. After an interval (which becomes shorter as the game progresses), the fish reemerge once again and pursue the paintbrush.

Each time in a given board that the player rollers a fish, he is awarded greater points—double the points from the previously rolled-over fish. These bonuses can be extremely important, since they reach as high as 9,000 points! The bonus points are as follows:

Figure 13-3

Bonuses for Rollering Fish

Board No.	1st Fish Eaten	2nd Fish Eaten	3rd Fish Eaten	4th Fish Eaten
1	50	100	200	400
2	100	200	400	800
3	200	400	800	1600
4	400	800	1600	3200
5	800	1600	3200	6400

5th Fish Eaten	6th Fish Eaten	7th Fish Eaten	8th Fish Eaten	9th Fish Eaten
800	1600	3200	6400	9000
1600	3200	6400	9000	
3200	6400	9000		
6400	9000			
9000				

During each board, a character appears, emerging from one of the houses. The character leaves marks or "trax" on the surfaces painted by the player. The player must destroy the character by hitting him with the paintbrush and cleaning up all the trax which were left by the character. The characters for the first six boards are a small cat, a mouse, a bird, a runaway tire, a large cat, and an invisible man.

When the board is totally painted, the character destroyed, and all trax painted over, the board is completed. A new board of identical configuration appears, and the game begins anew. The fish become more elusive and faster-moving in later boards.

In some games, a randomly placed black spot appears on the board. When the paintbrush encounters this spot, it will disappear and rematerialize at a random location on the screen (similar to the "hyperspace" feature on ASTEROIDS℠ and some of the other games).

Scoring and Number of Men

Painting the board: The player is awarded points as he paints the board. Although how the tally works is not listed on the game's instructions, points awarded are a function of the path lengths painted by the player. These points average about 2,500 points per board.

Painting over the trax:	10 points
Catching the character:	1,000 points
Rolling over the fish:	50 to 9,000 points, as shown previously.
Completing a board:	1,000, 2,000, and more points.

Most game settings give the player three paintbrushes (the game can be set up to six paintbrushes), with an additional brush awarded at a score of 10,000 points.

How You Lose

Only one way—when the paintbrush is eaten by one of the two fish.

Facts You Should Know

1. To speed up. The two rollers are located at one end of each of the two overpasses on the board. When the paintbrush hits the roller, it speeds up, increasing the distance between it and a pursuing fish.

2. The irreversible roller. Once the paintbrush starts pushing the roller across the overpass, the roller will continue its movement even if the player reverses. The roller sits at the end of the overpass where it was last pushed by the player.

3. Tie goes to fish. If you are pushing a roller and hit a fish with it at the very end of one of the overpasses, you, not the fish, are destroyed.

4. The fish have brains. The fish are smart and get smarter with each consecutive board. For example, they'll spot you entering a tunnel and slyly separate, one heading to each end of the tunnel, thereby trapping you.

5. The unpainted trap. Sometimes tiny portions of the board are left unpainted. The unsuspecting player will think he's completed a board and relax, waiting for the next board to appear, then find the fish still chasing him. Look for a little triangular-shaped unpainted surface, usually located at the edges of the board dividers, and paint it quickly.

Figure 13–4

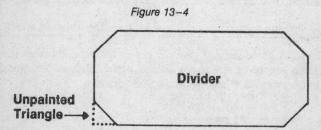

7. Strategies

Beginning Strategy

Your goal, as a beginning player, should be to clear the first board. Try to eat a moderate number of fish with the roller (four or so) and your score, including the 1,000 bonus at the end of the board, will be about 4,000 to 5,000. That's a good start.

Try to paint as much of the board as possible at the beginning of the game (and in fact at the beginning of each new paintbrush) while the fish are still waiting in their aquarium. The beginning pattern below seems to work in all machines I've played, to start the first and second boards.

Figure 13–5

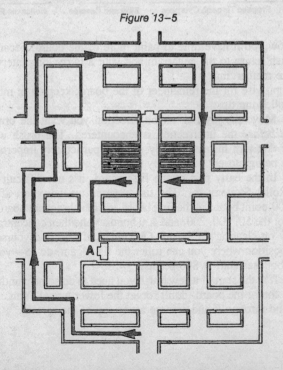

To make sure the pattern works, start the brush moving the instant the game begins, by holding the joystick to the left just after you push the START button.

Proceed left around the periphery to the top of the board. Head south and approach the lower overpass. Hesitate at the entrance to the overpass (point A), until the first fish is right on your tail. Then pick up the roller and go through the overpass. When you hit the other end, get on the other side of the roller and immediately reverse direction. You should be able to hit both fish with the roller, for bonuses of 50 and 100 points (we call this Roller Strategy #1).

Figure 13–6

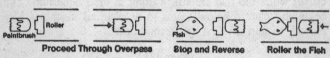

Paintbrush Roller

Proceed Through Overpass   Stop and Reverse   Roller the Fish

Fish

Now you'll have time to paint more of the board, because the fish return to the aquarium and wait a fairly long interval before reemerging.

Improvise for the remainder of the board, keeping in mind the following tips:

1. Move the joystick in the direction you want the brush to go *before* the intersection is encountered. The brush will make that turn instantaneously. This is particularly important when being closely pursued by the fish.

2. In the early part of the first board, it's not difficult to use Roller Strategy #1. The fish smarten up, however, after the 400-point bonus in the first board and in subsequent boards. Try for the 50, 100, 200, and 400 bonuses and then concentrate solely on clearing the board. Obviously, if you find yourself in a position where you can roller the fish again, do so—your next bonuses start at 800 points.

3. If at the start of a new brush you need to do some painting at the top of the board, don't forget the lower tunnel. You can descend through it and emerge at the top of the screen.

Advanced Strategy

The key to racking up high scores is to hit many fish with the roller during each board (particularly during the first board) and reap the huge bonuses that are awarded. For example, if you manage to hit eight fish during the first board, you'll get 12,750 points in bonuses alone. If you hit a 9th fish (a 9,000 bonus), your total bonus is 21,750!

As I said, the fish learn. After you hit them four or five times, Roller Strategy #1 rarely works. The fish will not pursue you into the overpass (or they'll back out of the overpass rather than follow you through it).

Sometimes you can entice them in by continuing forward after you reach the opposite end of the overpass, pretending that you will not reverse. Then when you see the fish in the overpass, reverse quickly and bop them. But this strategy is dangerous. If you proceed too far before reversing and get to the roller the same time the fish does, you'll be destroyed. (Always remember: *Tie goes to fish!*)

An alternative strategy (Roller Strategy #2) is to enter the overpass from the end opposite the location of the roller with the fish following you. Continue until you are just on the other side of the roller and reverse quickly, eating the pursuing fish.

Figure 13–7

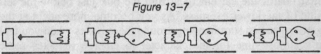

Enter Overpass with Fish Following   Stop and Reverse   Roller the Fish

A more sophisticated roller strategy (#3) is to enter the lower overpass from the end opposite the roller, with the fish behind you. To ensure that they follow you, continue straight across and enter the side tunnel. Emerge from the other side of the tunnel and enter the overpass once again. This time, however, when you get to the other side of the roller, reverse and bop 'em.

Be careful when trying Roller Strategy #2 or #3. The fish which is not pursuing you may proceed to the opposite end of the overpass and enter it, destroying you before you can reach the roller (or hitting you just as you reach the roller; once again, tie goes to fish).

Coordinated fish. The fish also use teamwork to get you — as if one knows what the other is doing. For example, they'll work together to trap you in the tunnels. As one pursues you into the tunnel, the other will advance to the other end of the tunnel, thereby surrounding you.

Keep the fish together. Try to keep the fish together as much as possible (by using delays and hesitations). When they are both at the top of the board, for example, and you're at the bottom of the board, you cannot be surrounded. Use your peripheral vision and try *always* to be aware of the location of both fish.

Use the rollers. When closely pursued, you may get away from fish by pushing the roller through an overpass — because you speed up.

Eating the characters. Each of the six characters comes out of its "home," the location of which is shown on the screen. Become familiar with these locations. For example, during the first board, the cat emerges from the box just below the left side of the lower overpass. As you become more adept at the game, you can start hanging around these boxes when you feel it's almost time for the character to emerge (it takes some practice to get this timing down). Then you can bop the character early in his life, preventing him from leaving many trax on the board, which, of course, you must paint over before clearing the board.

The characters are not nearly as elusive as the fish. But you rarely bop them by chasing them. They are best caught from the opposite direction, that is, by hitting them head on. They seem more susceptible to getting caught after you emerge from an overpass.

But don't become preoccupied with the character and ignore the fish. That's suicide!

14. THE STAR OF 1980: ASTEROIDS™

In 1979 and early 1980, most videophiles were playing SPACE INVADERS ™, in arcades, bars, and restaurants around the country. Gradually Atari's video star, ASTEROIDS, began replacing SPACE INVADERS, until by the summer of 1980, ASTEROIDS became *the* game to beat.

ASTEROIDS' popularity was due primarily to its fascinating theme (and despite the fact that its original screen was in black and white). But ASTEROIDS was also the first major game to offer two novel features which no doubt contributed to its becoming the star of 1980.

1. An ingenious ego-feeding feature was added, whereby the top players could record their initials, name, or nickname (up to three letters) on the screen for all the world to see. I and thousands of others continually fed quarters into the game so we could have our names recorded for posterity (or at least until the plug on the machine was pulled out) in our favorite bar.

2. The player was awarded an indefinite number of extra men, if his score warranted it.

1. Basic Objective

To stay alive as long as possible and, while so doing, to shoot and destroy as many (or all) of the asteroids and enemy saucers.

2. Scenario

Picture yourself in a spaceship, weightless in the middle of space. From 4 to 16 large asteroids are floating toward you;

if they collide with you, you are destroyed. You may shoot at them, but they only break down into smaller asteroids. Eventually, when they're small enough, your shots can destroy them. Every once in a while, enemy saucers, probably from Mars, approach you and fire at you, often with deadly accuracy.

3. Novice, Good, and Expert Scores

- Novice players rarely hit 1,000 points.
- Good players score from 5,000 to 15,000.
- Experts score in the 40,000 to 80,000 range.
- Nationally ranked players can score over 1,000,000.

4. Controls

Complexity rating: High.

The two ROTATE buttons on the left are used to rotate the player's ship to the left or to the right.

The FIRE button on the right is used to fire at the enemy.

The THRUST button on the right is used to move the player's ship in the direction in which it is pointing.

The HYPERSPACE button is used to make the player's ship disappear and reappear at a random location elsewhere on the screen.

Figure 14–1

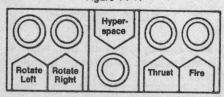

Most players use only the ROTATE buttons and the FIRE button. I would recommend this approach to beginners.

5. The Board

Figure 14-2

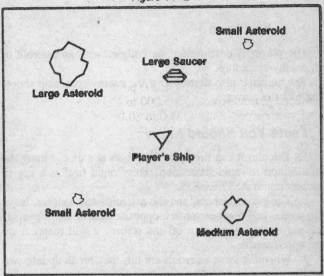

The bullets from the player's ship go in the direction in which the nose of the ship is pointing. The mission: to destroy the asteroids and the enemy saucers.

6. Characteristics

Scoring and Number of Men

Hitting a large asteroid:	20 points
Hitting a medium asteroid:	50 points
Hitting a small asteroid:	100 points
Hitting a large saucer:	200 points
Hitting a small saucer:	1,000 points

The player is given three men. He is awarded an extra man for *every* 10,000 points; there is no limit on the number of extra men.

The machine turns over at 99,990 points.

How You Lose

The player is destroyed if he collides with an asteroid or an enemy spaceship.

The player is also destroyed if the enemy spaceship shoots and hits the player.

Facts You Should Know

1. The player can fire up to four shots at a time, hitting the FIRE button in rapid succession. This "rapid fire" is a key to succeeding at ASTEROIDS.

2. The player's shots, and the asteroids and saucers, leave the screen and reappear on the opposite side of the screen. If the player thrusts his ship off the screen, it will reappear on the opposite side.

3. When the large asteroids are hit, they break up into two medium asteroids, which move in a different direction and at a different velocity. The medium asteroids break up into two small asteroids. The small asteroids, when hit, disappear. The direction and velocity of the resulting asteroids can sometimes be predicted after the player becomes familiar with the game. This is a key factor in skillful play.

4. Enemy saucers always enter the screen from the left or right side, never from the top or bottom. They do not start firing immediately (this allows them to be ambushed, as we will see).

The enemy saucers traverse in an irregular path across the screen, making erratic, elusive moves. Once they leave the screen on the left or right side, they are gone forever (until the next saucer appears).

5. The enemy saucers fire shots which can destroy the player. Once the saucer shots leave the screen, they are gone forever; they do not reappear on the opposite side of the screen.

6. In the earlier stages of the board, the large enemy saucers appear. They are easier to hit and their fire is not as accurate as that of the small saucers.

The small enemy saucers appear later in the board. They are more difficult to hit and their fire is far more accurate, which, of course, accounts for the point differential (1,000 vs. 200 points).

7. The first board begins with four large asteroids floating in from the edge of the screen. Successive boards begin with more and more large asteroids, until a total of 16 is reached.

8. If a player's ship is destroyed (and the game is not over), the space configuration continues uninterrupted, and the next player ship appears in the center of the board after a few seconds.

7. Strategies

Developing Hand-Eye Coordination for ASTEROIDS

Success at some of the video games depends on hand-eye coordination far more than predetermined strategy. Asteroids is one of these games. There are three things a player can do to ensure he is playing ASTEROIDS to his full physical capability:

1. Get to the point where you can turn your man by reflex, that is, as automatically as if you were riding a bicycle or driving a car. This training of your two fingers on the ROTATE button just takes repetition. You should start to feel comfortable with this after 10 games or so.

2. Become adroit at rapid fire. A very light touch on the FIRE button is required for this. You may fire in bursts of four, but you must hit the FIRE button for each shot. Some players believe that the best way to fire rapidly is to hit the FIRE button with the underside of the index and middle fingers held together (sort of like a congo drum player) rather than using the end of a finger as in most other games. Practice by hitting a flat surface four times, as fast as you can, either with the end of

a single finger or with the underside of the two fingers held together. Repeat this exercise over and over again.

3. Good peripheral vision is important in ASTEROIDS, since you must detect threats coming from several directions at the same time. Keep your face as far away from the screen as you can and still feel comfortable; this will increase the angle of your vision.

Beginning Strategy

Your first goal should be to get through the first board. At the beginning of the game, note which of the four large asteroids is most likely to float toward the center where you are located (usually only one). Shoot only at this asteroid.

Be aware of how the asteroids split into smaller asteroids and watch the change in direction and velocity. A large asteroid will split no matter where it is hit, so you have considerable latitude in where to aim. Leading a large asteroid and hitting it toward its front with one or two shots, followed by two more shots (you have four) aimed back where the center of the asteroid was, often results in hitting of resulting medium asteroids as well. This technique can also be applied to accomplish a medium-small asteroid parlay.

Beware of gratuitous shots at innocuous asteroids. You may find yourself unable to protect yourself (your four shots having been expended) against a subsequent threat. Try to anticipate which asteroids will pose a later threat to you by extrapolating on their current line of flight—they move in straight lines.

Note that your man is longer than he is wide. When threatened from the flank, you can often evade destruction by turning toward the threatening asteroid and stand by coolly as it floats right by you.

If you push the THRUST button and end up moving your man closer to the edge of the screen, you are likely to be destroyed. This is because you have the most time to react when in the center of the screen, where the machine first places you. Further, the accuracy of your shooting is far better when you're stationary. I strongly advise beginning and average-to-good players to stay in the center (i.e., avoid the THRUST button).

The HYPERSPACE button is a crapshoot. You never know where you may materialize on the screen—you might be destroyed immediately. It's the rare player who can hit this button by reflex in time to avoid an imminent threat. Obviously, if you know you're going to be destroyed (say, by two unavoidable attacking asteroids), you have nothing to lose by going for the HYPERSPACE button.

Advanced Strategy

In playing subsequent boards, you may be tempted to push one of the ROTATE buttons and fire as rapidly as you can, while waiting for the large asteroids to appear—in an attempt to get a "bead" on them. This destruction of large asteroids willy-nilly is generally bad policy because you'll find dangerous space matter floating around everywhere, increasing your risk.

If you're not faced with imminent threat from asteroids, always shoot the enemy saucer first. This is because it's shooting at you—often with great accuracy. As soon as you hear the distinctive sound announcing the presence of a saucer, locate the saucer, take a bead on it with appropriate "leading," and blast away as rapidly as you can.

Advanced players develop the skill of using the THRUST button by reflex and traveling around the screen while firing. This skill can be developed but it takes many games for most of us.

The ambush technique. This strategy, used by some advanced players, is designed to destroy as many saucers as possible during a given board—especially the small saucers, which are worth 1,000 points each. Here's how it works:

1. Destroy all asteroids but one.
2. Hit the THRUST button and direct your man to a spot about an inch away from the corner of the board (positions A or B).
3. Wait for the saucer to enter from the side.

4. When it does, quickly fire at it (you are safe; it does not fire at you when first entering the screen).

5. If it enters from the other side (i.e., you're lurking at position B and the saucer enters from the left), shoot into the edge of the screen, playing the angles (your shot will enter the opposite side of the screen). If the saucer threatens you, move your man off the edge of the screen (in our example, to the right) to safety on the other side. Then wait for the next saucer on the other side (in our example, at position A).

Figure 14-3

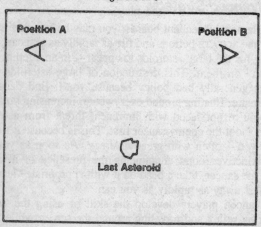

Final note. I've noticed that a given player's ASTEROIDS score can vary widely, more than in most games—due, it seems, to how "up" the player is. ASTEROIDS is definitely not a game for the imbiber; I've seen game after game last less than a minute, as the quarters (and drinks) are expended with amazing rapidity.

8. Other Versions.

ASTEROIDS DELUXE®. A "sequel" to ASTEROIDS was put out by Atari, no doubt to make the game more difficult as ASTEROIDians became more adept at the original game. As in the case of SPACE INVADERS PART II℠, another sequel, this game never became popular with players, most of whom felt the original game was far more fun. Further, ASTEROIDS DELUXE is a very difficult game to play.

The basic differences:

1. One of the most annoying differences is that the player's ship has been made larger and thus far more susceptible to destruction. Turning toward threatening space material no longer saves the ship.

2. The HYPERSPACE button has been eliminated. A SHIELD button which protects the player and which can be used to destroy the enemy by ramming has been added. Most players rarely use the shield; its another preoccupation in an already very busy challenge.

3. The game is essentially the same as ASTEROIDS, but there are a number of changes, including scoring values for different space matter, a limit (10) on the number of extra men, and increased shooting accuracy by the enemy saucers.

The good ASTEROIDS player can apply his skills to excel at ASTEROIDS DELUXE, but he will generally play for shorter periods of time. The ambush technique cannot be used because the saucers shoot at and destroy the asteroids we saved to keep the current board going.

15. TRAVELING TO THE MYSTERIOUS BASE: SCRAMBLE™

SCRAMBLE, like DEFENDERS™ and ASTEROIDS™, requires a high degree of hand-eye coordination. However, a knowledge of the features of this somewhat complex game and the deployment of predetermined strategies can lead the player to the achievement of respectable scores.

1. Basic Objective

To fly a little spaceship through five defenses, avoiding various obstacles and counterattacks along the way, in order to reach "the base." After destruction of the base, the whole sequence of defenses and obstacles starts over.

2. Scenario

You are in a spaceship, traveling in an alien land. The farther you penetrate enemy territory, the more menacing are the enemy defenses. Finally you reach the very core of the enemy, his headquarters or base, which you have an opportunity to destroy.

3. Novice, Good, and Expert Scores

- Beginning players rarely exceed a score of 2,000 points.
- Good players score between 5,000 and 15,000.
- Expert players can rack up 20,000 to 50,000 points.
- The very best players can get six-figure scores.

4. Controls

Complexity rating: High.

The four-directional joystick moves the ship vertically (the UP and DOWN positions) and from the extreme left side of the screen to the middle (the SLOW and FAST positions).

One button fires lasers, bullets which travel straight ahead.

A second button fires bombs, which travel forward and then down.

The stand-up arcade version has two sets of buttons to accommodate both right- and left-handed players. The sit-down lounge version has buttons only on the right-hand side.

Figure 15–1

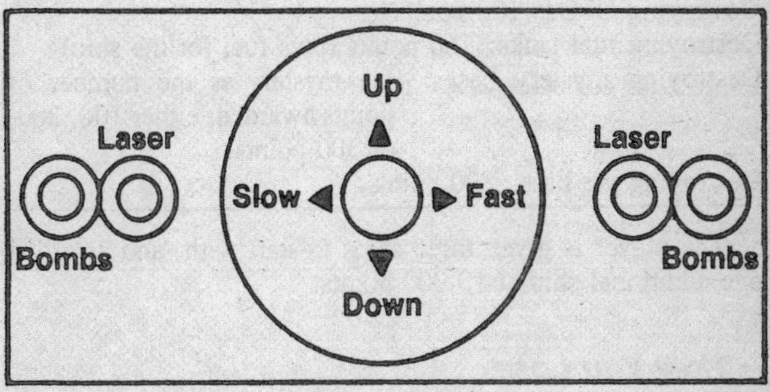

The background (i.e., the territory through which the ship is traveling) constantly moves from right to left at a constant speed. Moving the joystick to the left stops the ship's forward progress until the rear of the ship touches the leftmost edge of the screen. Then the ship is "pushed" forward at the same speed as the terrain.

If the joystick is moved to the right, the ship moves toward the center of the screen, traveling through the territory at a faster rate of speed than the basic velocity of the terrain. The ship cannot be moved farther right than the center of the screen. Full vertical control is available.

5. The Board

There are six board configurations, one for each of the five defenses and one for the enemy's base territory. Diagrams of the defenses are shown later.

6. Characteristics

Scoring and Number of Ships

Staying alive: 10 points per second
Destroying rockets: 50 points for grounded rockets
                       80 points for flying rockets
Destroying UFOs: 100 points
Destroying fuel tanks: 150 points (plus fuel for the ship)
Destroying mystery bases: the mystery is the number of
                              points awarded, either 100, 200,
                              or 300 points.
Destroying the base: 800 points.

The player is given three ships to start with, and awarded one additional ship at 10,000 points.

How You Lose

The player's ship is lost if:
• The ship crashes into something (whether a rocket, UFO, meteorite, the terrain, or anything else).
• Something crashes into the ship.
• The ship runs out of fuel (the amount of fuel remaining is shown at the bottom of the screen).

Facts You Should Know

Starting location of the ship. When the game starts, the ship is located in the center of the screen at the extreme left. Every time a ship is destroyed, the new one materializes on the screen at the same location, with a full tank of fuel. The terrain reverts to the beginning of the defense in which the previous ship was destroyed.

Fuel consumption. Fuel consumption is purely a function of time, totally independent of the speed of the ship, the number of bombs dropped or lasers fired, or the amount of ship maneuvering.

When fuel is very low, an ominous sound emanates from the game. If you run out of fuel, the ship will descend out of control until it hits something and is destroyed. Fuel is replenished by destroying fuel tanks. As the fuel tanks are destroyed, the fuel indicator shows by how much the fuel supply has been augmented.

The rate of fuel consumption increases in each new cycle of the six board configurations, up until the fourth cycle, after which it stabilizes.

Defenses. As mentioned, there are five defenses and a base territory. Each of the defenses is more difficult than the previous one. Traveling through the base territory and destroying the base is not as difficult as some of the defenses.

Player ammunition. The player may drop two bombs at a time and may not have more than two bombs on the screen at the same time. The player's ship is not hurt by the bombs, which in fact can pass through the ship without causing damage.

Lasers are fired in groups of four, but there is no limit on the number of lasers on the screen at the same time, so the player may keep firing indefinitely.

7. Strategies

At the beginning of the game and the start of each ship, move the ship to the center of the screen. It is generally advisable to keep the ship as close to the middle of the screen as possible, as this gives you more maneuvering room to drop back and speed up again to avoid enemy threats.

First Defense

The first defense, the easiest, consists of mountains and valleys, with rockets poised for takeoff interspersed among fuel tanks and mystery bases.

The rockets can take off at any time, necessitating quick reflexes to either destroy or avoid them before they hit and destroy the ship.

Figure 15-2

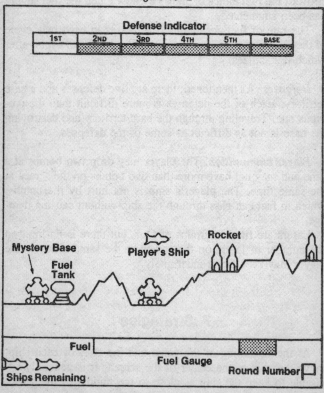

As you approach the first mountain (and subsequent mountains), drop bombs just before you reach the crest. You can lob them over the mountain, since the bombs move forward and then down. Don't be afraid to speed up and strike your own bombs; as I said, the bombs can't hurt the ship. Use the bombs to clear a space for the ship to enter by hitting the leftmost targets in the valleys. Then drop as close to the ground as possible, clearing your path by firing the laser continuously.

As you approach the last mountain of the first defense, drop two bombs to get the last fuel tank. Don't drop down to laser the tank, because you will most likely get zapped by one of the UFOs which will soon fill the screen in the second defense.

Second Defense

The second defense consists of swarming UFOs and smaller mountains and valleys, in addition to "mountains and valleys" at the top of the screen. As in the first defense, there are rockets, mystery bases, and fuel tanks along the bottom of the screen. The rockets do *not* take off in this defense.

To cope with the UFOs, stay at a constant height just above the mountaintops, firing lasers continuously. The vertically moving UFOs will eventually fly into a laser and be destroyed.

During this time, keep bombing, with fuel tanks as your top priority. This is because the ground-based rockets pose no threat during this defense and because it's better to go for a sure 150 points plus fuel than take a gamble on 100, 200, or 300 points from a mystery base. (Of course, when you get to be an expert, you'll be able to destroy practically everything.)

If a UFO gets by your initial laser shots, drop back and keep firing lasers. If you hit a UFO, race ahead and keep firing. If you miss again, wait until it gets close and then race by it.

Until you're very good, don't chase a UFO. You most likely will end up getting nailed by another one while trying to get the first one.

As you crest the last mountain of the second defense, the background changes color. *Drop down quickly* to avoid the meteors of the third defense.

Figure 15-3

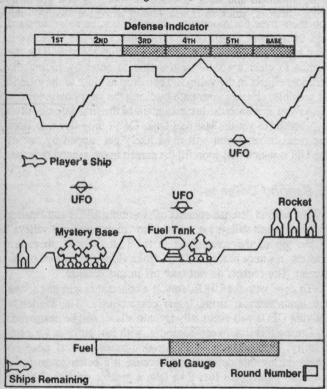

Third Defense

The third defense is identical in terrain to the second, except the UFOs vanish suddenly and are replaced by meteors. The meteors cannot be destroyed, so they must be avoided. The rockets do not leave the ground in this defense, so don't be afraid of them.

The third defense strategy is to drop down low, hiding in the valleys, until the way is clear of meteors. Then leapfrog the mountain and duck down once more. If you get caught out—that is, stuck in the middle of a meteor swarm—duck and dodge frantically and look for an opening to drop behind a mountain again.

The top of the screen has mountains as well, but don't hang around up there, because you'll periodically be forced into the path of the meteors and destroyed.

If you are destroyed during this defense (which you will be—it happens to the best of us), prepare for your next ship. It will appear where it always does, but in this defense, unlike

Figure 15—4

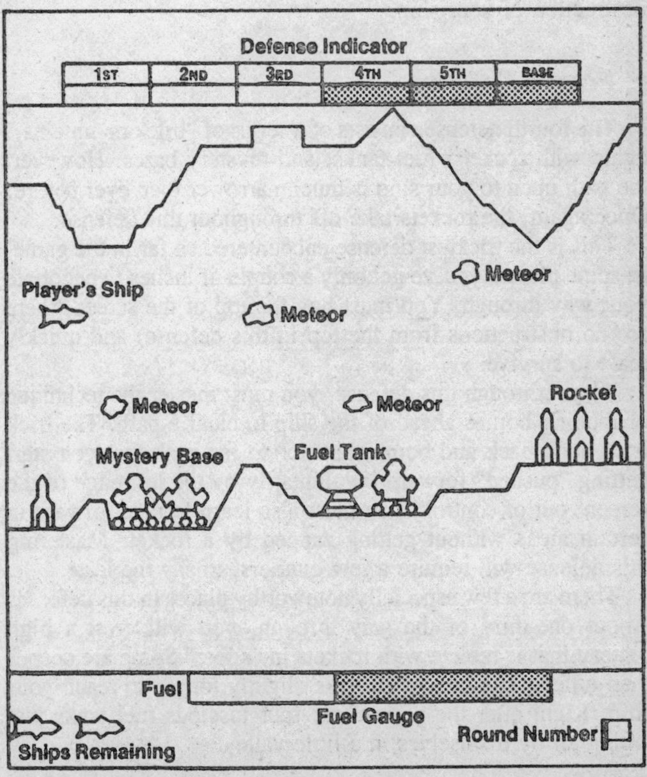

Defense Indicator					
1ST	2ND	3RD	4TH	5TH	BASE

Player's Ship

Meteor

Meteor

Meteor   Meteor   Rocket

Mystery Base   Fuel Tank

Fuel

Fuel Gauge

Ships Remaining   Round Number

the others, you don't have a few seconds of grace before the ship is imperiled. The meteors are right there, so be prepared for them and lower the ship as soon as possible. In fact, it's best to hold the joystick down *before* the ship materializes, so it starts descending as soon as it appears.

As you approach the end of the third defense, a multi-colored brick mountain appears at the right edge of the screen. Lob both bombs at the fuel tank and mystery base at the base of the mountain and climb up to crest the mountain. If you miss and try to laser these targets, you will not be able to gain altitude fast enough to avoid crashing into the side of the mountain. Even if you're low on fuel, it's better to gamble that you'll get a fuel tank later on than to accept almost certain destruction of your ship.

Fourth Defense

The fourth defense consists of a series of "brick mountains," again with rockets, fuel tanks, and mystery bases. However, the path open to your ship is much narrower than ever before. Once again, the rockets take off throughout this defense.

This is the trickiest defense encountered so far in the game. In some places, you've got only a couple of inches to negotiate your way through. You must hug the top of the screen (there are no obstructions from the top in this defense) and quickly react to survive.

To get through this defense, you must master the technique of lobbing bombs ahead of the ship to clear a path. The trick is to hang back and bomb, but not so far back that you start getting "pushed" forward involuntarily by the left edge of the screen, out of control. You must also learn to race forward in certain areas without getting zapped by a rocket. Mastering this defense will require a few quarters, to say the least.

There are a few especially noteworthy places in this defense. About one-third of the way through, you will crest a high plateau that is replete with rockets in "silos." Some are deeper than others, and hence will take slightly longer to reach your ship. Right after the plateau are four luscious fuel tanks just sitting all by themselves in a little valley.

Figure 15—5

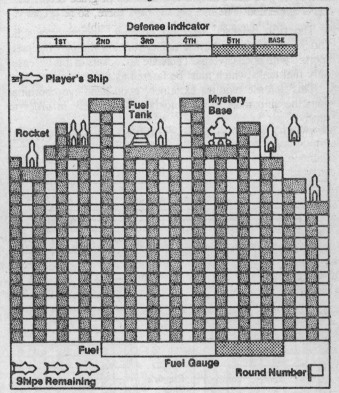

The greatest challenge is at the end of the plateau. The last rocket is extremely capricious about its lift-off time, and the fuel tanks cannot be totally destroyed if you either pass too high over or race by the rocket. The key is to be at exactly the right height and place, so that when you release two bombs, one will destroy the rocket and the other will destroy the first fuel tank. This clears a space for the ship to drop down and laser the entire plateau. Those who have achieved this have stated it is one of the sublime thrills of arcade gaming.

Fifth Defense

The fifth defense, the most difficult, comprises a solid "brick" wall with a narrow tunnel running through it, interspersed with open caverns. There are no rockets in this defense, only fuel tanks which must be lasered as the ship progresses.

This defense requires extremely good hand-eye coordination; the ship must move quickly and precisely in order to survive.

The key is (1) to race ahead at full speed while in a tunnel,

Figure 15–6

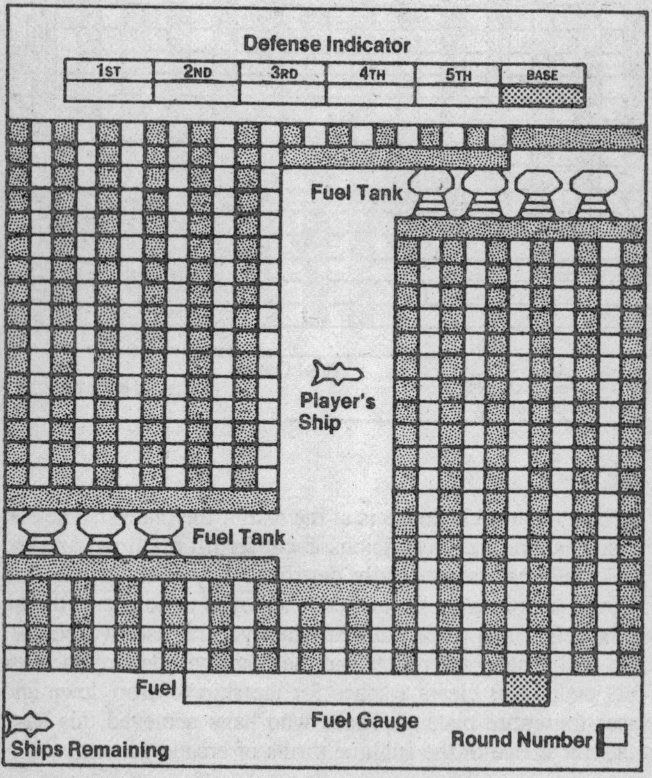

(2) to stop abruptly when exiting a tunnel, and (3) to go into full reverse and either full-speed ascent or full-speed descent in the caverns between tunnels. This will allow you to get to the mouth of the next tunnel without being forced into a wall.

Destroying the Base

After finishing the fifth defense, the player progresses into "base terrain," which is similar to the fifth defense except that there are no fuel tanks (or anything else). The mysterious base, which lies in a cavern (and subsequent caverns if not destroyed the first time), is sort of a let-down. It's just a little dome nestled between two tall brick towers.

The base may be either lasered or bombed. Race ahead to the center of the screen, raise the ship slightly (to avoid crashing into the tower, which is slightly taller than the tunnel), and drop down as fast as possible, keeping the rear of the ship almost touching the tower.

You will then encounter a shorter tower. Race forward, and drop down until you are in line with the base. Fire your laser, and *poof*, mission accomplished. If you prefer, after cresting the shorter tower, you can drop a bomb on the base instead. This will be necessary if the ship is too far forward to be put in line with the base in time. To bomb the base, however, you must be practically touching it, since bombs first go forward before dropping.

If you miss the first base, stay high in the screen and another set of towers with the base will come along. If you miss the second base, you probably will run out of fuel·before reaching the third.

After destroying the base, you won't be able to crest the next tower in time and will undoubtedly fly right into it. But (surprise!) it doesn't matter. You will be given credit for the ship, destroyed or not, and begin the next cycle anew, with a full tank of fuel. Then it's time to do all this all over again, but with a higher rate of fuel consumption.

Once you've destroyed the base, a congratulatory message appears on the screen. But start practicing—because I'm not going to tell you what it is.

16. THE DIVING, DODGING INVADERS: GALAXIAN™

GALAXIAN is sort of a spiffed-up version of SPACE IN-VADERS™. As in SPACE INVADERS, enemy aliens are arranged in formation; but they move more evasively, and they leave the formation to attack the player. The aliens can be quite intimidating until the player gets used to their attack patterns, which, it turns out, are somewhat predictable.

1. Basic Objective

To stay alive, by shooting enemy aliens and avoiding collision with them or their missiles.

2. Scenario

You are in a ship, presumably protecting a planet (although no terrain is displayed on the screen). Your ship can move only horizontally.

You are threatened by a formation of enemy aliens overhead. The formation moves elusively across the sky, making it difficult to draw a bead on the aliens. Periodically, aliens, usually from the ends of the formation, peel off and attack you, firing missiles as they descend. They swerve evasively in order to avoid your missiles.

The aliens that make it past you unscathed disappear below you. Then they reappear above and either rejoin the formation or continue their attack.

If all of your ships are destroyed, the world (and, even worse, your game) is ended.

3. Novice, Good, and Expert Scores

• Novices will probably not get through the first attack wave (we'll call them "boards" from now on) and will score up to about 2,500 points.

• Good players generally can complete 5 to 10 boards, scoring between 15,000 and 40,000 points.

• Experts get well into six figures. I've watched a player score 650,000 points (Joe from the Fascination Arcade in New York City), but have never seen anyone turn the machine over—i.e., score 1,000,000 or more points.

4. Controls

Complexity rating: Average.

A two-directional knob, which moves the ship to the left or right, is operated by the left hand.

Figure 16–1

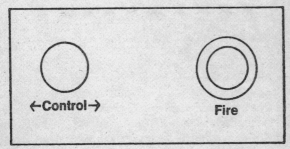

←Control→   Fire

A FIRE button is controlled by the right hand. Rapid fire is not usually required, since only one missile at a time may appear on the screen. As in SPACE INVADERS, the player may not fire another missile until the previous one has been expended, either by hitting something or by disappearing off the top of the screen.

5. The Board

Figure 16–2 shows the screen as it appears at the beginning of the first board. Even in Galaxia, RHIP (Rank Has Its Privilege):

• The lowest three rows of the formation are each made up of 10 blue Galaxians. These aliens are like Galaxian privates;

Figure 16–2

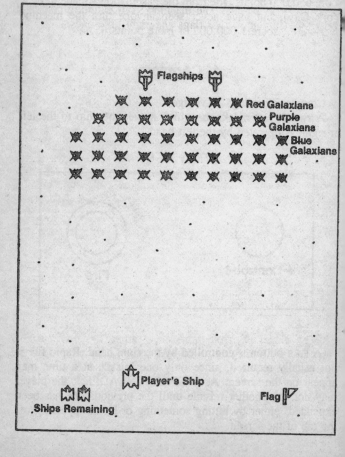

they're most subject to being hit by your missiles, and they're the least imaginative in their attack patterns.

• Next in rank are the eight purple Galaxians in the fourth row from the bottom, followed by six red Galaxians in the fifth row.

• At the very top is the brass—two Galaxian flagships. They have so much pull that when they attack, they are generally escorted by two red Galaxians.

Little flags in the lower right portion of the screen indicate which board is being played. A big flag with a 10 in it appears after every 10 boards. The machine stops counting boards at board 48 (staying at four flags and eight little ones).

6. Characteristics

Scoring and Number of Ships

Points are awarded for shooting Galaxians, as follows:

Blue Galaxian:	30 points in formation;	60 while attacking
Purple Galaxian:	40 points in formation;	80 while attacking
Red Galaxian:	50 points in formation;	100 while attacking
Flagship:	60 points in formation;	see below

Attacking flagship:	
If alone:	150 points
With 1 red escort:	200 points
With 2 red escorts:	300 points
If 2 escorts are destroyed first:	800 points

The player is given three ships; an extra ship is usually awarded at from 5,000 to 20,000 points, depending upon the game setting.

How You Lose

By being hit by any of the aliens or their missiles.

Facts You Should Know

Galaxian attacks. Galaxians fire at the ship only when they're attacking. Individual aliens usually fire three shots per attack trip. The flagship and its entourage of two red Galaxians usually squeeze off seven shots per trip. When the flagship is destroyed, its escorts no longer launch missiles.

As the player completes boards, the aliens attack more frequently, and they become more evasive in their movements. The attacking aliens alter their paths depending upon the location of the ship; as we shall see, the player can use this to his advantage.

The enemy formation. The formation moves across the board horizontally until its first column reaches the end of the screen. Then it reverses its direction. When it reverses, it is more difficult to fire accurately at the aliens.

Total points after clearing boards. There can be wide variations in the number of points scored after each board is cleared, depending primarily upon the number of flagship-entourage wipeouts the player accomplishes (worth 1,000 points each if the two red escorts are destroyed before the flagship). The following table gives a rough idea of how many points you may expect to score after completing each of the first 15 boards:

Figure 16–3

Waves completed	Cumulative points (thousands)
1	2–3
2	6–7
3	11
4	14
5	18
6	21
7	25
8	28

9	32
10	36
11	40
12	43
13	47
14	51
15	55

Strategies

Beginning Strategy

It is critical not to waste shots. A missed shot will render the ship impotent for the entire time it takes the missile to reach the top of the screen. Thus the player loses valuable shooting time. Make each shot count. While the strategy "if in doubt, shoot" applies to some games (such as TEMPEST® and DEFENDER®), it is not a sensible approach to GALAXIAN.

With a little experience, the player will get used to the horizontal movement of the alien formation and will be able to pick off one alien per shot. When the formation reaches the end of the screen, however, it reverses and the tempo of the game is changed.

Therefore, concentrate on shooting the extreme columns of the formation. This will minimize these reverses.

Shooting aliens horizontally. Adjust your tempo to the movement of the formation. Fire, hesitate, fire, hesitate, etc. The hesitation should be just long enough for an alien from the next column to be hit. The correct timing should come to you after only a few games.

Shooting aliens vertically. Move the ship with the formation and fire, destroying aliens in the same column. This strategy should be used when shooting out the extreme columns. Again, with concentration, the correct tempo should come to you after a few games.

You obviously must give priority to attacking aliens, for two reasons: (1) they're the only ones firing at you, and (2) you're awarded more points for destroying them. It should also be obvious that the earlier you shoot them, the better—again for two reasons: (1) they will not be able to fire at you any longer, and (2) they don't bob and weave as much when they first leave the formation.

If an alien is getting close to you and you're having trouble catching him, try the "Don't shoot until you see the whites of his eyes" strategy. Track the alien and wait as long as possible before firing. If you wait until the very last instant, you know he won't dodge anymore, and he's yours. This approach takes courage, though. But if General Custer did it, so can you (let's hope you have better results).

Rapid fire will be required when you encounter the flagship and entourage. Try to shoot one red escort and then line up the other escort with the flagship. Blast them both in rapid succession. If you succeed, you've got 1,000 points.

Advanced Strategy

Watch someone else play a few games and observe the attack patterns of the aliens. While there are variations and they become more complex in later boards, notice that the aliens *do* have habits.

Blue Galaxians. They often fly in a flat question-mark pattern. They usually peel off in the direction opposite that in which the formation is moving and swoop down diagonally

Figure 16–4

across the screen. Some typical blue alien patterns are shown in Figure 16-4.

Purple Galaxians. They swoop at greater angles and are the trickiest of the aliens. Sometimes they even leave the screen and return (Figure 16-5).

Figure 16-5

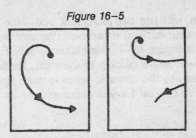

Red Galaxians. They serve primarily as escorts to the flag-ship. When they attack individually, they often begin like the blue aliens and then reverse direction, as in Figure 16-6.

Figure 16-6

Loops. Blue, purple, and red aliens are all capable of loop-ing and dangerously swooping into the base of the screen at a narrow angle. About all you can do is to try to anticipate where they will end up and get out of there fast!

Jiggling. Try an experiment. When there's only one alien left, jiggle the ship back and forth rapidly (avoiding alien missiles, of course). Just before the alien reaches you, perform one last jiggle. You should fake the alien out most of the time.

This is a good way to amaze your friends and get more time (but not necessarily that many more points) for your quarter.

Finally, as in several other games, there's a "loop" in the GALAXIAN program. With only one blue alien remaining, you can sometimes navigate the ship to the far left of the screen in such a way that the alien and his missiles will miss you continually.

The alien will fire two bombs at you—the left one will barely miss you, but you'll survive. The alien will follow the path shown in Figure 16-7. One caution—if he fires *one* bomb instead of two, move quickly to the right, let the bomb pass by, and return to the leftmost position once again. You can probably keep this up for just about as long as you feel like it.

Figure 16-7

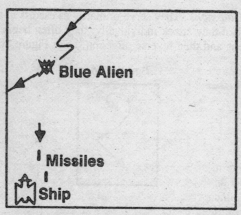

17. A QUITE PENETRABLE FORTRESS: STAR CASTLE™

There are many players around the country who can beat this game in every sense of the word, racking up millions of points and having dozens, and in some cases hundreds, of additional ships to spare. Yet the game remains confounding to the beginning player until its secrets are unlocked.

1. Basic Objective

To penetrate a "castle" of concentric rings and blast a cannon residing in the center, while avoiding three flitting buzzers and deadly firebombs fired by the cannon.

2. Scenario

You are in a spaceship, traveling through space. You spot a castle of three concentric rings protecting a centrally located cannon, which tracks your ship's location. You must penetrate the three circles by firing missiles at them and creating an opening through which you may fire at the cannon. When an opening develops, however, the cannon fires firebombs at you with deadly accuracy.

3. Novice, Good, and Expert Scores

• Novices who don't understand the game may get wiped out after only several hundred points.

• Good players can score between 20,000 and 50,000 points.
• Experts can play indefinitely, scoring millions of points and quitting the game voluntarily with many additional ships still to be played.

4. Controls

Complexity rating: High.

Two buttons which turn the ship either to the left or right are on the left side of the control board. On the right are two other buttons: the left one is a THRUST button, which moves the ship through space. The right button, the FIRE button, shoots missiles at the enemy (you may fire up to three missiles in rapid succession, and there may be a maximum of three missiles on the screen at one time).

Figure 17–1

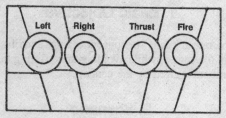

It takes a while for the player to be comfortable with the four controls. The expert player must know instinctively where each button is and be able to employ each almost subconsciously. Players who have become adroit at ASTEROIDS® can learn STAR CASTLE rapidly because the controls are identical (except that STAR CASTLE has no HYPERSPACE button). To give you an idea of the "learning curve" here, it took my friend Raymond seven weeks to be able to score millions of points at ASTEROIDS; when STAR CASTLE subsequently came out, it took him only two weeks to crack the game.

5. The Board

In the middle of the board is the cannon surrounded by three rotating concentric circles:

- The inner ring moves counterclockwise.
- The middle ring moves clockwise.
- The outer ring moves counterclockwise.

Each ring has 12 segments. When a segment is hit by our missile the first time, it lights up. The second time it's hit, it disappears.

Figure 17–2

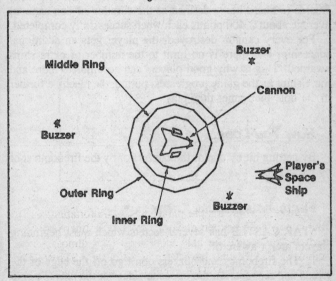

The screen itself is all one color—blue. But colored circular overlays are superimposed over the center of the board. This creates the illusion that the outer ring is red, the middle one is orange, and the inner one and the cannon are yellow.

6. Characteristics

Scoring and Number of Men

Destroying a segment (i.e., hitting it twice) of the rings, as follows:

Outer ring:	10 points
Middle ring:	20 points
Inner ring:	30 points

For each cannon destroyed: a bonus of about 2,000 points. Boards (a board being defined as the duration of one cannon) average about 2,400 points each when successfully completed.

For every cannon destroyed, the player gets an additional spaceship, and there is no limit to the number of extra ships awarded. This is why good players can accumulate more and more ships as the game progresses, putting the machine further in the hole the longer they play.

How You Lose

By getting hit by one of the buzzers or by the firebomb shot by the cannon.

Facts You Should Know

STAR CASTLE has several secrets which most beginning players aren't aware of:

1. The firebombs and buzzers don't go off the edge of the screen and reappear on the opposite side, but the player's ship does. (There are exceptions to this. In some boards, on some machines, a buzzer occasionally materializes on the opposite side of the screen with the spaceship.) The player's missiles also travel "inter-screen."

2. Contrary to one's natural tendency, it is much better *not* to blast away willy-nilly at the ring segments to expose the center as soon as possible. We will soon see why this is so.

3. The player's ship almost never gets blasted if it keeps moving fast enough.

Cannon and fireballs. The cannon tracks the ship less accurately in early boards, but with deadly accuracy in later boards, flipping almost instantaneously into a position aimed directly at the ship. When there's an opening through all three rings, it releases a firebomb, which fortunately is not of ICBM quality—its trajectory is a straight line. We are warned of the firebomb's existence because it makes an electric-sounding noise.

The rings. When all segments of the outer ring are destroyed, the segments of the middle ring move outward, replacing the outer ring (which in turn is replaced by the segments of the inner ring). A new inner ring is formed.

When the ship hits the castle, it bounces off the outer ring segments back into space—even if no outer ring segment exists (it's as if the destroyed segment left an invisible shield in its place—a shield which deflects only the ship, but not the missiles).

The buzzers. The buzzers originate within the castle and flit around the board. They often take a rest and attach themselves to the outer ring. They can be destroyed if hit by player missiles, but the player gets no points for this. Thus buzzers should be shot only as a defensive measure. In later boards, the movement of the buzzers becomes quite tricky.

The defenses. As the boards progress, the castle defenses speed up: The rings rotate more rapidly, the cannon tracks the ship more accurately, and the buzzers flit more dangerously. Here are several notable spots at which the defenses change:

- Around the fourth board, the rings rotate a bit faster.
- Around the sixth board, the buzzers flit somewhat more dangerously.
- Around the eighth board, the cannon tracks the ship a bit more accurately.
- At about 80,000 points, the cannon reaches its maximum tracking accuracy.

- At about 100,000 points, the rings, buzzers, and cannon all move at peak velocity.
- At about 180,000 points, inexplicably, all three defenses slow down to a snail's pace.
- At around 210,000 to 220,000 points, the defenses are back up to maximum speed again.

A training secret. The defense "slowdown" phase comes at about every 180,000 points—that is, at around 360,000 points, 480,000 points, and so on. This allows for an unusual training opportunity. The expert player can take the game up to 180,000 points (or 360,000 points, etc.). Then he can turn the game over to the novice, who can train against weak defenses with 40 to 60 free ships at his disposal. This training would cost him $10 to $15 if he started from scratch.

Strategies

Beginning Strategy

The beginning player will tend to shoot out ring segments as rapidly as possible in order to amass points. This is absolutely the wrong approach.

In order to destroy the cannon (and get the bonus, another ship, and another board), be discriminating about which segments of the rings are destroyed. If the entire outer ring is destroyed, it will be replaced by the segment configuration of the middle ring, which does not further our objective of establishing an opening to the cannon.

An effective beginning strategy is as follows:

1. Shoot at contiguous segments of the outer ring until about half of the outer ring remains (see Figure 17–3).

2. Fire shots into the castle through the removed portion of the outer ring. Be careful not to hit any more segments of the outer ring. Eventually enough segments of the middle and inner rings will be destroyed so that you have a straight shot to the cannon.

3. When an opening to the cannon develops, watch out!

Figure 17–3
Shooting the Outer Ring

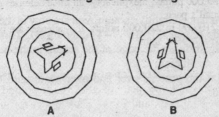

A   B

Keep moving the ship to avoid the firebombs that will be coming your way, rapidly and accurately.

4. When safely out of the way of firebombs and buzzers, blast away at the castle. (Once again, avoid hitting the remaining segments of the outer ring.)

5. If you dodge well and fire accurately, the castle will eventually be destroyed (it will take you a few games to get used to the operation of the four buttons).

Using the corners. You can take advantage of the fact that the ship and missiles go inter-screen but the firebombs and buzzers (for the most part) do not by using the following strategy:

1. Locate the ship in a corner of the screen, facing the edge of the screen (Figure 17–4, diagram A). Experiment with the inter-screen angles so you are able to fire missiles into the castle from this position.

Figure 17–4
Using the Corners

A   B   C

2. When threatened by buzzers or a firebomb, lightly tap the THRUST button so you go inter-screen, avoiding these threats.

3. If you tapped lightly enough, you are now in the opposite corner of the screen (Figure 17–4, diagram B). Turn the ship so it once again faces the edge of the screen in the new corner (Figure 17–4, diagram C).

4. Repeat the process over and over again until the castle is destroyed.

A shooting tip. When firing, tap the FIRE button three times as rapidly as you can (a light touch really helps), thereby releasing the maximum of three missiles and wreaking the most havoc upon the enemy.

Advanced Strategy

Once you've become comfortable with the controls, it's time to move on to advanced STAR CASTLE strategy:

1. Get the ship moving in two diagonal paths across the screen (Figure 17–5). If you do this correctly, you will traverse the screen alternatively on path A, then path B, then path A, etc.

2. When on path B, start shooting into the castle at point C. First destroy about half of the outer ring.

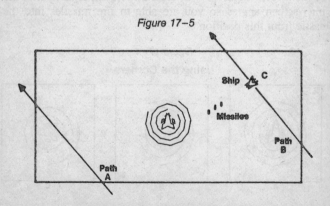

Figure 17–5

3. Every time you're on path B, fire three shots into the castle (avoid hitting the remaining portion of the outer ring). Observe the rotational speed of the outer ring and adjust your thrust timing so the ship enters the screen on path B just as the existing portion of the outer ring rotates out of your firing path.

4. When you're comfortable with steps 1 through 3, start firing three shots at the castle when on path A as well, doubling your destruction efficiency.

5. When you get the timing down so that each time you enter the screen, whether on path A or path B, the outer ring has rotated out of your shooting path, you have joined the ranks of STAR CASTLE masters and should be able to play the game indefinitely.

Raymond, using this technique, racked up 2,001,980 points and walked away from the game, leaving 476 unused spaceships behind him!

18. THE GAME THAT STARTED IT ALL : SPACE INVADERS™

SPACE INVADERS was by far the most popular video game in 1979. Its popularity continued into 1980 until it was gradually replaced by ASTEROIDS™. There was a craze for this game, including a SPACE INVADERS song, T-shirt, and thousands of devoted addicts, which was second only to the current mania over PAC-MAN™.

My roommates and I became so hooked on "Vader's" as it is called, that we purchased a game (for $1,500). The game was kept running at least four to six hours a day by us and others who dropped in to play. After several months, and hundreds of games, we were scoring between 20,000 and 70,000 points.

1. Basic Objective

To stay alive as long as possible. A secondary objective is to amass extra points by shooting down the spaceships that periodically appear and traverse across the top of the screen.

2. Scenario

Picture yourself standing on earth all by yourself defending your civilization against 55 attackers from outer space, who are continually descending toward you, closer and closer, making threatening thumping noises. They're all shooting at you, and one hit will destroy you. If you let any of the attackers reach earth, the world is over. Talk about responsibility!

There are 55 enemy men, arranged in five rows of 11 each,

continually firing at us, the lone defender at the bottom of the screen. We are protected by four barriers (called "the green"), which are gradually eroded as they are hit by enemy bombs. We can traverse left or right, hiding behind the green and shooting at the enemy men, who are destroyed after being hit once.

The enemy moves across the screen. When they reach the end of the screen, the men descend one level lower and begin to move in the opposite direction. The enemy keeps descending level by level, and the men turn "half-green" when they get a moderate distance from the bottom and "full-green" when they get close to the bottom.

As more of the enemy men are shot, they move faster and faster. When there are few of the enemy remaining, they rapidly traverse the screen, making it difficult to destroy them. The player must "lead" them by estimating the time it will take his shot to reach the enemy.

After all the enemy men are destroyed, a new board appears with 55 more attackers. The game becomes more difficult, because the new men appear one level closer (lower) to us, giving us less time to destory them. On each successive board, the enemy appears continually lower, until the 10th board, when the men appear on the same level as the second board and the process begins anew (the men revert to the second level on the 18th, 26th, 34th, and every eight boards thereafter).

3. Novice, Good, and Expert Scores

- Beginning players rarely hit 1,000.
- Good players generally score between 3,000 and 8,000.
- Expert players hit between 12,000 and 50,000.
- Nationally ranked players have scored 100,000 and higher. The machine turns over at 9,990.

4. Controls

Complexity rating: Average.

There are two basic controls:

• Buttons to move the player to the left and the right, on the left side of the control board, best activated by the player's middle and index fingers (left hand).

• A FIRE button on the right side of the control board, best activated by the middle or index finger of the right hand.

The player may not fire another shot until the previous shot has either hit a target or passed beyond the top of the screen. Thus the player must be aware of the disposition of his previous shot, so he'll know exactly when he can fire the next shot.

Figure 18—1

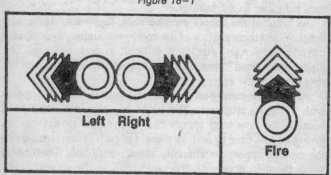

5. The Board

The board below shows the enemy men as they appear at the beginning of the first board. The player, at the bottom of the board, is protected by the four green barriers. The spaceship periodically appears and moves across the top of the screen.

Note the location of the word SCORE and of the score for the first player. Specific letters and digits in these will later help us in timing the shooting of the spaceship.

Figure 18–2

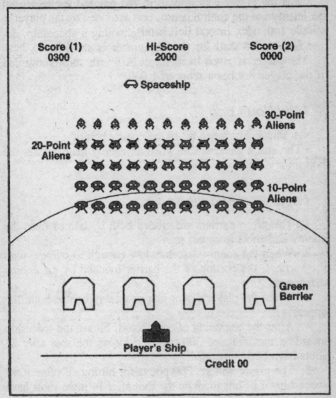

Score (1)
0300

HI-Score
2000

Score (2)
0000

Spaceship

30-Point
Aliens

20-Point
Aliens

10-Point
Aliens

Green
Barrier

Player's Ship

Credit 00

6. Characteristics

Scoring and Number of Ships

• 10 points for shooting enemy men in the bottom two rows.

• 20 points for shooting enemy men in the third and fourth rows from the bottom.

• 30 points for shooting enemy men in the top row.

Thus the player gets a total of 990 points for clearing all 55 enemy men in each board.

50, 100, 150, or 300 points for shooting a spaceship, depending, as we shall see, on the number of shots fired.

The player is given three ships. A fourth ship is awarded if the player reaches a score of 1,000.

How You Lose

• A ship is lost when hit by an enemy bomb.

• The entire game is lost when an enemy man reaches the bottom level of the screen.

Facts You Should Know

1. The green barriers are eroded both by bombs from the enemy and shots from our man.

2. When the enemy descends low enough to overlap with the barriers, the portion of the barrier touched by the enemy disappears.

3. When the player's shot hits an enemy bomb, both disappear.

4. After the beginning of each board, hitting the spaceship awards a maximum of 300 points if hit on the shot after 22 shots have been expended.

5. The player will get 300 points for hitting all subsequent spaceships if he hits them on the shot after 14 more shots have been expended. (This point and the previous one are key to advanced play, as we shall see).

6. Spaceships appear as a function of time rather than as a function of the number of shots taken or enemy men destroyed. Thus the advanced player must often wait for spaceships to appear.

7. Spaceships do not appear if there are eight or fewer enemy men on the board.

8. When enemy men are on the second row from the bottom, they do not fire bombs (this permits an advanced method of play, called the "green method").

9. There are nine levels on which the enemy men appear at the beginning of the board, as follows:

Level no.	Color of lowest row of enemy men
1, 2, 3	White
4, 5, 6	Half-white and half-green
7, 8, 9	Green

7. Strategies

Beginning Strategy

Your first goal should be to clear the first board, after which you will have a score of 990 points, plus the bonus points received for hitting spaceships.

The beginner should be concerned only with shooting all 55 of the enemy men. He should ignore the spaceships until he can clear the first board with ease.

The enemy bombs are easy to duck if the enemy men are high on the screen. When they get lower, the player often panics, makes hasty movements, and is destroyed.

There are two ways to keep the enemy from getting too close to the bottom. One is obviously to shoot the lowest enemy men in their formation. But a second key way is to shoot out the vertical rows on the extreme right and left side of the enemy formation. This is because the enemy will not drop a level until one of its men touches the end of the screen. If the enemy formation is narrow, then the enemy must make more lateral moves on the screen before reaching the end of the screen.

Thus the player should aim at:

1. Enemy men in the lowest row (labeled A in the diagram).
2. Enemy men in the extreme columns (labeled B in the diagram).

As more enemy men are destroyed, the enemy moves faster and faster. The player must shoot in front of ("lead") the enemy more and more. This timing cannot be taught; it comes from learning the tempo of the game through continuous play. Natural ability also enters in here—some players (probably those with shooting-gallery ability) are far better at leading the enemy than others.

Defensively, the player must watch the enemy bombs. It's usually easy to duck the bombs in the first board. If the situation gets tight, the player may duck behind one of the green barriers until danger passes.

It is safest to shoot for the sides (rather than the center) of the enemy men. This gives you more time to move out of the

Figure 18-3

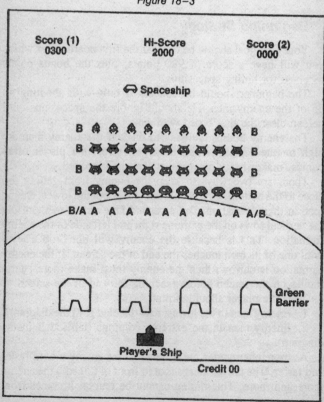

way. Watch advanced players. Note how they "shoot-and-slide," moving the man to the (say) left, taking a shot, and immediately moving the man back to the right. It's sort of like in the old western movies where the cowboys peer out from behind a rock, take a shot, and duck back to safety. The same principle applies in Vaders.

Try to develop this shoot-and-slide technique. It will become handy, indeed necessary, in advanced play when the enemy men are firing at you fast and furiously from the lower levels of the board.

Advanced Strategy

The player who can clear the first board without difficulty has two ways to go to increase his score. The first is to start "counting", as it's called—that is, counting the number of shots so he can get 300 points for each spaceship cleared. The second is to work on the shoot-and-slide technique to be able to handle advanced boards. We'll discuss each of these in turn.

Counting. Count the number of shots starting at the beginning of the board. For the first grouping, it's best to clear several vertical columns (I do the left three columns) on the end of the enemy formation. Then fire shots into space or into the "green" until your count reaches 22. Then go over to the right of the enemy formation and wait between the two green barriers on the right—actually exactly halfway between the E and D in the word CREDIT at the bottom of the screen. After a few seconds the spaceship will enter the screen from the right. Shoot it as soon as you hear its noise. You should hit it dead on, and you will be awarded 300 points.

Then shoot some of the enemy men in the lowest row; if you shoot four or fewer of them, the enemy men will not speed up, which is to your advantage. Continue to count; waste a few shots until your count reaches 14. Then wait between the left-most barriers on the screen. After a few seconds, the spaceship will appear from the left. Shoot it as soon as you hear its noise. Another 300 points!

Then shoot a vertical column on the end of the formation.

Figure 18-4

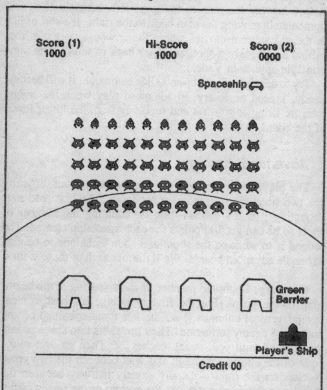

Score (1)
1000

Hi-Score
1000

Score (2)
0000

Spaceship

Green
Barrier

Player's Ship

Credit 00

Waste some more shots until your count reaches 14. Then move your man to the extreme right of the screen. Wait there until the spaceship appears on the left of the screen. Do *not* shoot until the spaceship is exactly between the s and the c in the rightmost word SCORE above it (see Figure 18-4). Then shoot. 300 points!

Shoot another vertical column and fire into space or into the green until your count reaches 14. Then move to the extreme left side of the screen. Wait for the spaceship, which will appear at the right side of the screen. Wait until the space-

Figure 18-5

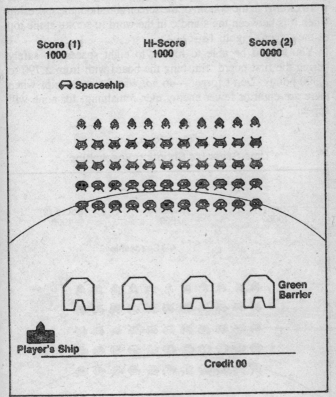

ship is directly under the last digit (always O) of the first player's numerical score (Figure 18-5). Shoot, for another 300 points.

Repeat this process several more times, shooting at enemy ships in extreme vertical columns and at ships in the lowest row (as in beginning play). Go to the right side of the board and await the spaceship. All future spaceships in the first board will appear on the left and travel to the right. When it gets between the s and c (Figure 18-4), shoot it and collect your 300 points each time. To gain some time, when you become experienced, you may keep your ship waiting over the R in the word CREDIT at the bottom of the screen and shoot the spaceship when it is between the S and C in the word HI-SCORE at the top of the screen (Figure 18–6).

You should be able to hit six to eight spaceships safely during the first board, finishing the board with from 2,790 to 3,390 points. Don't forget—do *not* wait for spaceships when there are eight or fewer enemy men remaining, for none will appear.

Figure 18–6

Time-Saver for Shooting Spaceships

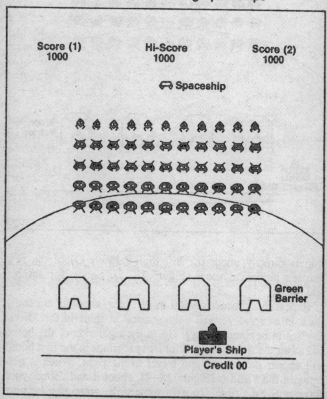

It becomes progressively more difficult to hit 300-point spaceships with each successive board. Go for fewer spaceships on each new board. It's better to preserve your man than to get a few hundred more points. When the fifth board appears (the second half-green board), it's best just to shoot the enemy men and forget about the spaceships entirely.

Shoot-and-slide. The shoot-and-slide technique becomes really important when the enemy men start turning green. Develop a rhythm. Most right-handers seem more comfortable hiding behind a barrier, moving right, shooting, and then moving left. This requires two-hand timing, pushing, in turn, the left index finger, the right middle finger, the left middle finger. A good practice technique is to sacrifice a few games and just practice shooting out enemy men as rapidly as possible, forgetting about spaceships and score. Develop your shoot-and-slide technique by letting the enemy get to the half-green and full-green levels before shooting at them. With some practice, you'll be quite satisfied with the dexterity you'll develop.

The green method. A technique we've developed for later boards is to leave one enemy man at the far left and let four or five columns of the enemy at the far right descend to the second level from the bottom of the screen (the level at which they don't fire bombs). As the formation moves to the far right of the screen, move your man to the far right and traverse to the left, shooting out the bottom row of the enemy. Then wait for the enemy to move to the right and move to the far right and repeat the process.

This process can work, but is dangerous, because it's difficult to finish up the enemy at the far left. Don't experiment with the green method until you're totally comfortable with the other Vaders techniques discussed here.

8. Other Versions

SPACE INVADERS PART II®. As players became more adroit at SPACE INVADERS and tied the games up for long periods for just one quarter, the manufacturer came up with a more difficult version. This version, as was the case with ASTEROIDS DELUXE®, never became popular with players, who, I guess, felt they were being ripped off by the complexities of the new game.

The basic differences:

1. After the first board, some of the enemy men split into two small men when hit. These men must also be destroyed before the board is completed.

2. The spaceship flashes during its right-to-left trip across the top of the screen. This makes it more difficult to hit, since half the time it's invisible.

3. Periodically in later boards, additional enemy men are added to the formation, making the player's task more difficult.

4. The graphics are more colorful and the board the player is playing is displayed in each of the barriers. Despite these improvements, the game did not catch the fancy of the arcadians as did the original version.

One strategy is exactly the same as for the original game, except that the player has more motivation to shoot for random spaceships in later boards when he is not counting, to get the higher bonus points.

19. HOME VIDEO GAMES AND PORTABLE TABLETOP GAMES

Home Video Games

The home video game market is currently exploding just about as fast as any industry in the country. Industry spokesmen estimate that sales of home video game products will be $3 billion in 1982.

The three major home video systems available to the player are the Atari VCS, Mattel's Intellivision, and Odyssey² from Magnavox.

Atari VCS

Atari dominates the industry, accounting for 75% of the sales of home video products. The Atari system is a sensible investment for those who enjoy variety in their games, for several reasons:

• Atari has the largest, most varied game library and offers cartridges of several of the most popular arcade games, including SPACE INVADERS™, ASTEROIDS™, and PAC-MAN™.

• Other companies are manufacturing cartridges to be used in the Atari system, including Activision, which sold $5 million in cartridges in its first year (1980) and is estimating 1982 sales of $50 million. Atari cartridges are also planned by Coleco, Inc., Imagic, Inc., and Apollo, Inc.

Atari's game controls consist of joysticks and paddles, which are plugged into the console. The console is a sturdy unit which can withstand the heavy punishment to which it is inevitably subjected by enthusiastic players.

Intellivision

Mattel's Intellivision is the Avis of home systems, but the system is a distant second, with about 15% of the market. Players generally agree that the Mattel system has the best color and graphics of all the systems. Their cartridge selection is limited, but growing rapidly. Coleco and Imagic plan also to produce cartridges for the Intellivision system.

Intellivision controllers are attached to the console; each has a circular control disk and four fire buttons. If you're into sports games, this system will probably appeal to you the most (there are cartridges for baseball, basketball, soccer, hockey, and auto racing). The game detail and the high degree of player actions are unsurpassed. My roommates are hooked on their baseball game, which they play for hours on end.

Odyssey²

Odyssey was the first manufacturer to produce a home video system, first made available in 1973. The original system was somewhat crude, and Odyssey was technologically leapfrogged by other manufacturers. However, Magnavox subsequently introduced the Odyssey² system, which is on a par with the others. Odyssey controls, which take the form of joysticks, are permanently attached to the console.

Odyssey² has a wide selection of cartridges, including several that excel:

• THE QUEST FOR THE RINGS™—a popular cartridge that was rated the most innovative by *VIDEO Magazine* in its 3rd Annual Arcade Awards.

• UFO™—rated the best science fiction game by *VIDEO Magazine*.

• K. C. MUNCHKIN™—a maze game similar to PAC-MAN.

Home Video Game Cartridges

A number of the more popular arcade games have been made into home cartridges.

PAC-MAN—(Atari).The home PAC-MAN game is not nearly as exciting as the arcade version. The concept of the home game is similar to the arcade game, with a player pursued by monsters who become vulnerable when energizers are hit.

The monsters are light in color and flash on and off, making them difficult to spot. Their color changes, as in the arcade game, but the change is subtle and difficult to observe. The joystick does not have the tight feel of the arcade game and doesn't allow for subtle controlled movements by the player. The board is oriented horizontally, rather than vertically, and there are no changing symbols with differing point values. I played the game for about an hour last month at the Consumer Electronics Show in Las Vegas before passing on to some of Atari's more interesting games.

K. C. MUNCHKIN—(Odyssey²). This is a maze game, similar to PAC-MAN. The player's "Munchkin" is pursued by three "Munchers." The Munchkin eats 12 little squares, "Munchies," which travel around the maze. If the board is cleared, the player is faced with another one, more difficult to complete.

SPACE INVADERS—(Atari). This cartridge is an exciting adaptation of the grandfather of the arcade games. The aliens travel across the screen and drop bombs on the player's ships. There are a number of game options, and SPACE INVADERS can be played by either one or two players.

ASTEROIDS—(Atari). This cartridge was introduced in the fall of 1981 and became an immediate success. The games (there are several options) are exciting, and the color and graphics are excellent. The game was selected by *VIDEO Magazine* as the best home game of the year in their 3rd annual Arcade Awards contest.

PORTABLE TABLETOP GAMES

PAC-MAN—(Coleco). Coleco introduced a portable version of PAC-MAN in early 1982. In addition to conventional PAC-MAN, the game offers head-to-head PAC-MAN—where two players compete with each other in eating dots and monsters, and Eat-and-Run—where the player tries to maneuver PAC-MAN out of the center box to eat energizers and return safely to the center box.

The games are exciting, and, as in the original versions of PAC-MAN, patterns can be developed to complete boards.

GALAXIAN™—(Coleco). Also introduced in early 1982, this game is really three games in one. In addition to conventional GALAXIAN, similar to the arcade game, there is head-to-head GALAXIAN—where two players fire missiles at each other's fighters and defenders, with a time limit. Also included is ATTACKERS™—where the player must elude missiles dropped by attackers on the player's defender.

GALAXIAN II™ and SPACE INVADERS 2™ (Entex). Entex has developed hand-held games which are also quite similar to the arcade versions. The games are designed so two players may play simultaneously, each on a different side of the board.

ABOUT THE AUTHOR

Ken Uston is widely known as the foremost blackjack player in the world. He has been featured on *60 Minutes* (February and May 1981), the *Today* show, *Good Morning, America, The Tom Snyder Show, The Mike Douglas Show, That's My Line,* and *To Tell the Truth.* Feature articles about him have been included in *The New York Times Magazine* (cover story), *Time, Newsweek, Sports Illustrated, People, Money, US* and countless other periodicals.

Ken is no stranger to teaching methods. He has written four books. His most recent, *Mastering PAC-MAN,*® has been listed on *The New York Times* Best Seller list. His best-selling book on blackjack, *Million Dollar Blackjack,* has been acclaimed as "the most complete book ever written on the game of blackjack" (*Boardwalker* Magazine). His first book, an autobiography entitled *The Big Player,* is being made into a major motion picture.

Ken is a Phi Beta Kappa Bachelor of Arts in Economics from Yale University and an MBA from Harvard University, and has been teaching blackjack around the world for the past five years. He has been Senior Vice-President of the Pacific Stock Exchange, Director of Operations Research for the Southern New England Telephone Company, and a consultant for Cresap, McCormick and Paget, and has also taught several courses in Business Management at Quinnipiac College in Hamden, Connecticut.

As Ken puts it, "Mathematical and logic challenges of all kinds have always been of interest to me, whether it's computer programming, probability analyses, bridge, blackjack, PAC-MAN or the other video games."